TH

B.

FREEDOM PRESS CENTENARY SERIES
Supplement to
Volume 2, SPAIN AND THE WORLD

To the memory of

CAMILLO BERNERI
(1897-1937)

and all the victims of
the counter-revolution
in Catalonia, May 1937

Cover by Rufus Segar

THE MAY DAYS BARCELONA 1937

Augustin Souchy · Burnett
Bolloten · José Peirats
Emma Goldman

FREEDOM PRESS
LONDON
1998

Published by
FREEDOM PRESS
84b Whitechapel High Street
London E1 7QX

1987, reprinted 1998

The Chapter *Barcelona: The May Events* by Burnett Bolloten
is reprinted by kind permission of the author and the
University of North Carolina Press, publishers of *The Spanish
Revolution*© 1979

ISBN 0 900384 39 5

Printed in Great Britain
by Aldgate Press, London E1 7RQ

CONTENTS

CAMILLO BERNERI
(1897-1937)
Murdered by the Stalinist
counter-revolutionaries, Barcelona
May 5 1937

EDITORS' PREFACE

One of the few books about the May Days in Catalonia 1937 is by Manuel Cruells,[1] at the time a working journalist on the Barcelona daily *El Sol*. What is specially interesting about this book is that it was published in 1970 in Barcelona five years before Franco was officially declared to be dead. It is a disappointing work because he extensively quotes from writers who were not eye-witnesses instead of concentrating on his own reports and recollections as one who was. However, in the opening chapter in which he attempts to place the May Days in their historic perspective he expresses his amazement that they should have virtually gone unnoticed by "many historians of the social movements of the twentieth century" and that when they do refer to the May Days in Barcelona in most cases it is "to present them as minor incidents in the Spanish Civil War".

This certainly sums up the reactions of the academic historians in the English speaking world. Any student of the Spanish Civil War today must rely on two major works on the subject — by Hugh Thomas[2] and Gabriel Jackson[3] and two historians of anarchism — by Professors Joll[4] and Woodcock[5] and will be disappointed if s/he hopes to be enlightened on the momentous events of May 1937. I will refer at greater length to these works in the Bibliographical Epilogue, but suffice it to say here that Professor Lord Hugh Thomas in his massive 1,100 page *History* gives eight to the May Days (and if one allows for his imaginative, colourful adjectives and irrelevant footnotes, actual facts about the May Days reduces the eight pages to about two); Professor Gabriel Jackson dismisses the whole business in just over a page of his 578 page volume, referring any reader who might have had his/her interest aroused to Broué and Temime for "the best short account of the Barcelona events". Professor Joll in the 1964 edition of his work on the anarchists gives a couple of pages to the May Days but prefaces his account with the comment "How or

why it started is still extremely obscure". In the second edition of
his work published fifteen years later and described by the
publishers as a "revised edition of a widely acclaimed and very
important work" the Professor is still unable to shed light on the
May Days and in the Index they are still referred to as having
taken place in 1936. George Woodcock's *History of Anarchism*
(1962) has now also appeared in a second edition (1986). Like Joll
he refers readers to others for a detailed account of the Civil War,
but it is with some satisfaction that we note that at last after 25
years and eight reprints he has excised the recommendation:
"especially in Hugh Thomas' admirable recent history"! But in
fairness to Professor Woodcock the half page he can spare to the
May Days of 1937 is a reasonable summary of those events. Unlike
most academic historians he refers to the "governmental *coup* of
May 1937" (the author's italics) whereas most refer to the
'uprising' or, as the communists say, to the 'putsch'. However in
view of the superficial treatment of these events their conclusions
are equally superficial to say the least. Woodcock sums it all up
with "From that time the CNT ceased to count in the Spanish
scene", or Thomas' "The 'May Day' of Barcelona showed that the
anarchists could not be counted upon to respond as one to any
situation". Professor Joll in both editions assures us that "the
consequences to the anarchist movement in Spain were far graver
than the loss of many individual militants". One heartily agrees
but he, even in the second edition doesn't tell the reader why! And
it is understandable that Professor Jackson, who could only spare a
page, draws no conclusions but proceeds immediately to the
Caballero government crisis. As to the Communists (who after all
have done more by their propaganda to influence the historians in
their approach to the Spanish Civil War) their official line[6] is to
describe the May Days as "the unsuccessful putsch carried out by a
section of the anarchists and the members of the POUM (usually
regarded as Trotskyist) in Barcelona in May 1937 [which] has been
the pretext for a vast amount of misrepresentation which has given
this episode a greatly exaggerated position in the history of the
Spanish War".

   The purpose of this small volume is to break the conspiracy of
silence and historic distortion so far as the momentous events of
May in Barcelona are concerned. All the material in the pages that
follow is now out of print. The most important contribution is
Augustin Souchy's account based on an hour by hour diary which

was first published as a four page supplement to the fortnightly anarchist journal SPAIN AND THE WORLD in June 1937 and in various translations at the time but which have been out of print for at least forty years. Burnett Bolloten's valuable chapter from his *magnum opus*[7] supplements Souchy's report with the comings and goings of the politicians, which in retrospect confirms Souchy's on-the-spot account. And since the Communist official line is to dismiss accounts of the activities of NKVD agents (the Russian secret police) as being 'apocryphal', I have added material on *The Counter-revolution on the March*, including an article by Emma Goldman giving details of her visits to political detainees in Republican prisons. A short chapter from José Peirats *Anarchists in the Spanish Revolution* (1977) is included to provide background material of the months leading up to the May Days. In the Bibliographical Epilogue I have included a page from his book summing up his views on the compromises made by the CNT-FAI in the months leading up to the final compromise by the leadership during the May Days of Barcelona 1937. Many anarchists, this writer included, would certainly endorse his sentiments.

NOTE

The following abbreviations have been used in the text to identify organisations and political parties:

CNT (*Confederación Nacional del Trabajo* — National Confederation of Labour). The revolutionary syndicalist organisation influenced by the anarchists.

FAI (*Federación Anarquista Iberica* — Anarchist Federation of Iberia).

FIJL (*Federación Iberica de Juventudes Libertarias* — Iberian Federation of Libertarian Youth).

MLE (*Movimiento Libertario Español* — Spanish Libertarian Movement). The combined CNT-FAI and FIJL.

UGT (*Union General de Trabajadores* — General Workers' Union). Reformist Trade Union controlled by the socialists.

PSO (*Partido Socialista Obrero* — Workers' Socialist Party).

PCE (*Partido Comunista Español* — Spanish Communist Party).

PSUC (*Partido Socialista Unificat de Catalunya* — Catalan Unified Socialist Party). The combined Socialist and Communist Parties of Catalonia.

POUM (*Partido Obrero de Unificacion Marxista*). Dissident revolutionary Communist Party.

1

Prelude to the May Days
José Peirats

By the beginning of 1937 the new State was ready to take on the revolutionaries. Until then its motto had been, 'The war must be won before the revolution.' Now its motto became, 'Before the war is won the revolution must be crushed.' A leader of the Unified Socialist Party of Catalonia (PSUC) had declared, 'Barcelona must be taken before Zaragoza.'

The revolution was represented by the CNT-FAI, the left wing of the Socialist Party and the Marxist Workers Unity Party (POUM). The counterrevolution included the Communist Party and its affiliates, the regional and national Republican parties and the right-wing Socialists led by Indalecio Prieto. Whatever their fundamental differences, the latter groups were united by their opposition to the revolution. Communists and anarchists opened hostilities on May 3, 1937.

There are those who claim that the events of May were part of a vast scheme to overthrow the President and Minister of War, Francisco Largo Caballero. Largo Caballero himself believed that the Communist offensive was directed only against himself. In his book, *Mis Recuerdos*, he writes, 'The Communist ministers took advantage of the May events to precipitate the crisis in the government that they had long been preparing.' In fact, the scheme was even more ambitious, for it was an attack on the entire revolution. If the objective had been merely the government in Valencia, then why did so much happen in Catalonia? The answer, of course, is that Barcelona was the stronghold of the CNT-FAI, which led the revolution. The anarcho-syndicalists controlled the Catalan government. Their unions and collectives had a strong

11

influence on the economy, and their war industries and militia columns at the front affected the progress of the war.

A systematic bid to take over the State began August-September, 1936, when Marcel Rosenberg and Antonov-Ovseenko became, respectively, USSR Ambassador and Consul-General in Spain. In coordinated operations, the Ambassador, with Communist Party help, worked to impose Russian policies on the central government; the Consul-General, with PSUC help, worked on the Catalan government to the same end. The Republic's diplomatic isolation and the Soviet military aid facilitated their operations. The Soviet aid was not disinterested: since December, 1936, the gold reserves of the Bank of Spain had been held in Moscow as security for commercial transactions between the two countries.

The Communists turned against Largo Caballero when he resisted the Soviet Ambassador's political and military meddling. Also, he had rejected a proposal for merging the Socialist and Communist Parties into a single workers' party called the Unified Socialist Party of Spain (PSUC).

In December, 1936, Stalin sent a personal letter to Caballero with insolent political advice, telling him to protect the petty bourgeoisie and put an end to the revolution. His pretext was the need to reassure the western democracies belonging to the Non-intervention Pact. In February, 1937, Stalin wrote again to Largo Caballero, openly proposing the formation of a single proletarian party. Caballero's reply to the first letter had been courteous but evasive. The second response was a flat refusal. The Spanish Communist Party immediately opened fire.

After his experience with the merger of the youth groups and formation of the Unified Socialist Party of Catalonia, Caballero knew what to expect. He, the 'Spanish Lenin', was destroyed by the agit-prop. Caballero wrote, 'The portraits disappeared everywhere. They took pleasure in destroying the idol they themselves had created.'

On February 8, 1937, the propitious moment arrived: Malaga fell to the enemy. At once the Communists produced a propaganda campaign playing on the emotional aspect of the disaster. They chose as scapegoat General Asensio, Largo Caballero's assistant in the Ministry of War. Unlike Generals Miaja, Rojo, Pozas and others, Asensio had refused to join the Communist Party. The campaign against him seemed to punish him for his refusal to toe the Communist Party line and to subvert the authority of the head of government and Minister of War.

At the same time, Caballero's personal enemies within the Socialist Party and UGT worked to isolate him from his own party. On February 24, 1937, his friends protested publicly that a number of Socialist Party activists had been detained without the knowledge of the regular police. In mid-April anarchist newspapers denounced a rash of assassinations of peasants by 'persons carrying CP cards'. Shortly before, in late March, there had been a clash between the collectivists of Vilanesa (Valencia) and the police, after a protest against the commercial tariff policies of the government. The police exceeded their authority, assaulting and destroying the collective's headquarters, in spite of the peasants' fierce resistance. At the same time Francisco Maroto, anarchist commander of militia on the Granada front, was accused of complicity with the enemy. The source of these allegations was the Governor of Almeria, Gabriel Morón, a Communist masquerading as a Republican. Maroto had made several forays into enemy territory, including the city of Granada, which the enemy had held since the first days of the uprising. The Communists based their charges of high treason on these incursions. The National Committee of the CNT came to Maroto's defense, 'If Maroto entered Granada, it is because he was more skilled than Morón, "the hero of Almeria".' Maroto was condemned to death, but his sentence was commuted. In 1939 he was shot by those who won the war.

April 20, 1937 saw the abscess that had been sapping the strength of the Madrid Junta of Defense burst. The Junta had been formed from all parties and unions when the government abandoned Madrid in November, 1936. Within it, the Communist Party gave full rein to its sectarian intrigues. Its Counselor for Public Order was José Cazorla, a former Young Socialist, now a Communist in the JSU like Santiago Carrillo and others. Cazorla detained a youth who turned out to be nephew of the Undersecretary of Justice, Mariano Sánchez Roca. For seventy days the fate of the youth was unknown until Melchor Rodríguez, special delegate for Prisons, learned he was being held in a Communist Party 'cheka' (secret, unofficial prison) on calle Fernández de la Hoz. This sensational discovery led to others. It was said that Cazorla was ransoming prisoners to get money for the Party. The government took advantage of these accusations to

dissolve the Junta of Defense on April 23 and instal a Municipal
Council in its place.

The scandal of the 'cheka' had only begun. The existence of
another, that in Murcia, was made public. *Castilla Libre*, the CNT
paper, published this note:

We have not opposed, nor will we oppose the shooting of any
fascist, whoever he may be. But we will always be opposed to
torture. Yet not only fascists were tortured in Murcia. Members of
revolutionary groups and Popular Front parties were sadistically
tortured in its infamous secret prison. Even a CNT member...suf-
fered the terrible torture of having his eyes torn out before his
wounded body disappeared.

The Socialist Party press joined the protest campaign, for many of
its members had also been tortured in Murcia.

The dissolution of the Madrid Junta of Defense embittered the
campaign against Largo Caballero. He responded with decrees
that purged police forces of Communist Party members. He wrote
in his book,

I issued another decree revoking the appointment of all
Commissioners named without my signature. One of those most
responsible had been Alvarez del Vayo, Minister of State,
member of the Socialist Party, and Commissioner (General), who
until then had been my unconditional friend. He called himself a
Socialist but actually he was entirely in the service of the
Communist Party. I made him appear before me; I reproached
him for his conduct and for the appointments made without my
knowledge and signature, which numbered about 200 in favour of
the Communists.

From that moment the Communists sought a successor for the
head of government. In his book, *I Was Stalin's Agent*, ex-general
Walter Krivitsky reveals.

Caballero was then universally considered the Kremlin favourite,
but Stashevsky had already picked Negrín as his successor because
Caballero had not supported the GPU activity which under
Orlov's direction had begun in Spain, as in Russia, a great purge of
all dissidents, independents and antistalinists whom the party
lumped together under the name 'Trotskyists'.

A counterrevolution accompanied the political changes. On November 26, 1936, CNT and UGT national representatives had signed a preliminary agreement that seemed to foreshadow an alliance between the two federations. The Communist Party claimed there was a conspiracy of labour unions against the political parties, in particular the Communist Party. The Republican parties took the bait, and the right wing of the Socialist Party renewed negotiations with the CP for a Single Proletarian Party.

Shortly afterward, the first division within the Catalan government was instigated by the Soviet Consul-General. He published a note accusing the POUM paper, *La Batalla*, of 'selling out to international fascism'. That note, brazenly abusing consular prerogatives, contained a synthesis of all successive slanders against the POUM. It was published on November 27, and the crisis of the Catalan government occurred on December 13.

The PSUC declared that it would end the crisis only if the POUM was excluded from the government. This purge served as a preliminary to the physical elimination of POUM leaders and also as the first move against the CNT and FAI. Throughout the world Communist parties were engaging in 'anti-Trotskyist' purges, a persecution began when Kirov was 'assassinated' in 1934. These sectarian struggles were only part of the Stalinist hostility to the POUM: there was also competition for control of the unions. The POUM had a great influence in the Catalan UGT, to which it had given life long before the creation of the PSUC. After July 19, 1936, the parties opposing the CNT had given the UGT a new image and from then on it would find its strength in the petty bourgeoisie. The Stalinists had to eliminate POUM influence in UGT unions. Hence, the crisis in the Catalan government was instigated to eliminate the POUM politically.

The crisis was resolved on December 15, by the creation of a 'government without political parties' formed by the UGT, CNT, Sharecroppers' Union, and the Republican Left of Catalonia representing the petty bourgeoisie. There was hardly any change in people: Comorera and Valdés, who had represented the PSUC in the government, now represented the UGT. It was they who had precipitated the crisis; they were the same characters in different costumes. But the POUM had been eliminated.

In the new government the different departments were redistributed. The Supply Department passed from the hands of

CNT member Domenech to the Communist Comorera (secretary general of the PSUC) who immediately began a slanderous campaign against his predecessor. He stepped up rationing of articles of primary necessity, especially bread, and attributed chaos in the bread industry and a scarcity of flour to the previous administrator and collectivization. The truth is that large quantities of goods were stored away to provoke public protest. When the people protested, Communist agents started rumours that the CNT was responsible for the bread shortage, and this led to well-orchestrated demonstrations against the CNT.

About that time, on January 20, 1937, a Soviet ship arrived at the port of Barcelona with a declared cargo of 901 tons of wheat, 882 tons of sugar, and 568 tons of butter. The people in the street joked a lot about the butter, since it was hardly ever used in Spain. They let themselves believe the 'butter' was really guns and planes. Even though it was confirmed in official circles that it was real butter made from cows' milk, nobody believed it. Lower government officials themselves ended up believing that the Russians had disguised war materials in order to circumvent the controls of the Non-Intervention Pact. The truth is that the Russians never unloaded war materials in Barcelona, but rather in Alicante or Cartagena, far from the anarchist columns. The Russian government bolstered the reputation of the Catalan government's new Councillor for Supplies with these shipments of foodstuffs.

Another accomplishment of the new government of Catalonia was the reorganization of the police. On December 24, The Councillor for Internal Security, a Communist named Artemio Ayguadé, appointed as a new Police Commissioner a PSUC member, Eusebio Rodríguez Salas. The new commissioner quickly began a campaign against 'uncontrolled elements' who, according to him, were undertaking unauthorized investigations and executions. · Another of his sensationalist campaigns was against the so-called 'clandestine cemeteries', really the burial places for rebels killed on the first day of the rebellion. Executions like these had taken place throughout the republican territory and all the parties and groups had participated, above all the Communists, who now wanted to lay the blame on their political rivals. To make a better impression on foreign observers, Rodríguez Salas went about digging up the bodies and encouraging funeral processions of widows and other family members. The rebel radio, especially Radio Sevilla, took great pleasure in commenting on the macabre activities of the new Police Commissioner. These intrigues also were ultimately directed at the CNT-FAI.

On January 23, 1937, the Catalan UGT, guided by the PSUC, held a 'congress' of small peasant landowners. The congress, really a propaganda stunt against the collectives, was run by non-peasant Communist speakers. These shady tactics soon bore fruit among the smallholders opposed to collectivisation. They took arms in La Fatarella, a small village in Tarragona, and were harshly repressed by the Control Patrols, a kind of mobile police formed by all the parties and groups in August, 1936. The punitive action of the patrols aided by the Assault Guards of the Catalan government left 30 dead among the smallholders, and several dead and wounded patrolmen. Responsibility for the event was collective, but the PSUC leaders sought to blame it entirely on the POUM and the CNT.

The conflict between the two sides escalated and a few isolated incidents occurred on the streets of Barcelona when the police of Rodríguez Salas tried to disarm all civilians. The Councillor for Internal Security, apparently on his own initiative, decreed the following: the dissolution of the Internal Security Corps formed by all antifascist groups; the dissolution of the Councils of Workers and Soldiers charged with purging the ranks of the old officer corps; the dissolution of the Control Patrols; and the prohibition of policemen, officers and police chiefs from belonging to unions or political parties, under penalty of expulsion. These decrees appeared on March 4, and their publication precipitated a new government crisis in Catalonia.

About this time, ten armoured cars were stolen from the warehouses of the war industries of Barcelona. The robbers were discovered to be high officers in the Vorochilof barracks, which was controlled by the PSUC. *Solidaridad Obrera* of March 7 commented,

If they did not remove the tanks to take them to the front, why was such a brilliant operation undertaken at all? We assume that this was the first step in a dictatorial coup, against which, everybody know , we would immediately rise.

The new government crisis was precipitated on March 26. As a solution the CNT demanded strict observance of the principle of proportional representation when departments were distributed. It also demanded the revoking of the Decrees of Public Order. A FAI communiqué said, 'The Department of Supplies should serve the interests of the people as a whole, not those of the parties. And Internal Security should not be filching that which is essential to the revolution in progress.' The crisis lasted one month, and while it was under negotiation there were moments of dangerous tension. On March 30, the CNT Regional Committee instructed its activists, federations and unions to keep alert and in constant contact.

Another cause of the crisis was the Communist campaign against the Councillor of Defense, the CNT member Francisco Isgleas. He was blamed for the lack of offensive operations on the Aragon front. We have already pointed out that on the Aragon front there was a great lack of weapons and, above all, ammunition. Nevertheless the leaders of the Communist Party presumptuously called the anarchist militiamen cowards. The Communists also slandered Catalan war industries which had been created precisely for the purpose of protecting the militia in Aragon from the sometimes intentional indolence of the central government. After Bilbao, Barcelona was the main centre for heavy industry in Spain. The war industries were mounted under the exigencies of war. Their products were sent to all of the fronts of the Republic. Workers and technicians of the CNT devoted all their skill and professional expertise to the enterprise. It was a true product of the CNT unions.

In a congress organized by the Young Communists in Madrid at the beginning of April, 1937, the speakers cast slurs on the Aragon front, arguing that its paralysis was attributable to its being 75% anarchist. Without any justification, the JSU Secretary General declared that there existed in Catalonia magnificent war factories given over to the production of pistol bullets. Other speakers added that Catalan war factories were making domestic appliances instead of machine guns and rifles. These allegations were amplified by the official papers of the CP, *Mundo Obrero* (Valencia) and the PSUC, *Treball* (Barcelona).

As we have seen, the government crisis in Catalonia lasted exactly one month. It ended on April 26 with the same cabinet as the previous government and a suspension of the Decrees of Public Order. But the incidents had only begun.

On April 25, 1937, in a town near Barcelona called Molins de Llobregat, a mysterious murder took place. At a crossroads, persons unknown fired on an automobile and killed its occupant, the PSUC activist Roldán Cortada. This murder served as a pretext for arresting a number of anarchists in the Bajo Llobregat district. To understand better the mysterious circumstances surrounding the crime, one should know the following:
1.   The Bajo Llobregat district was one of the most pro-anarchist in all Catalonia. During the revolutionary movements of January 8 and December 8, 1933, libertarian communism had been proclaimed in Hospitalet de Llobregat, the headquarters of the district committee.
2.   The anarchists of Bajo Llobregat had always distinguished themselves by the extremism of their revolutionary fervour. Barcelona conservatives accused the workers of this district of being anti-Catalan, because many of them had emigrated from different regions of Spain, especially Murcia. For the same reason, anarchists of Hospitalet were labeled 'Murcians' and 'foreigners' by Catalanist politicians.
3.   After July 19, 1936, Bajo Llobregat had been very heavily collectivised.
4.   When the CNT joined the government, the militants of Bajo Llobregat, true to their radical anarchism, formed an opposition movement to the CNT-FAI participation and the militarization of the militia. They published the journal *Ideas* in Hospitalet de Llobregat which objected to any deviation from libertarianism.
5.   In spite of intensive police investigations, Roldán Cortada's murderers could not be found. Nevertheless, several militant anarchists were detained and tried, including Luis Cano, Councillor for Defense of the Town Council of Hospitalet de Llobregat. The judge found Cano and his companions not guilty of the assassination and stated, 'With respect to the central issue of the indictment, neither the aforementioned Cano nor the six prisoners released had any part, direct or indirect, in the Cortada murder.' Cano was convicted only of 'exercising functions limited to the Department of Internal Security'.
6.   Let us see who Roldán Cortada was. In the old days he had been a CNT member. Like many other militants, he had taken refuge in France during Primo de Rivera's dictatorship. Afterwards he went to Switzerland, possibly expelled from France like many others who conspired there against the dictatorship. On

the eve of the fall of the dictatorship he returned to Spain secretly to continue the struggle against the military regime. In the first years of the Republic, Cortada worked very actively in the Construction Union of Barcelona and was one of the 30 signers of the dissident manifesto in the 1931 schism. Finally, after the military revolt of July 19, Roldán Cortada entered the PSUC, making a name for himself by his attacks on his former comrades.

With these facts we can advance the hypothesis that Roldán Cortada may have been assassinated by the Stalinists themselves to create enmity against the CNT. The site chosen for the attack — an extremist stronghold — makes motives for the attack seem self-evident, especially since Roldán Cortada was a renegade who might have betrayed the secrets of his former organisation when he joined the Communists.

The opposite hypothesis is difficult to sustain. The indicting judge found no evidence of anarchist participation in the crime. Furthermore, in all CNT history there were very few cases of reprisals against its renegades and these few were only against the gunmen of the Free Unions who, paid by the government, had assassinated CNT members such as Salvador Seguí, Evelio Boal, José Comas and the CNT lawyer, Francisco Layret. The reprisals took place in the first weeks of the revolution, and the main victims were Ramón Sales, Inocencio Faced and Desiderio Trillas.

The mere act of going over to the enemy had never brought about reprisals. Some of the Communist leaders had once been anarchists. Joaquín Maurín and Andrés Nin were the founders of the Communist Party in Catalonia, although they later deviated from the orthodox line. Ramón Casanellas had taken refuge in Russia after participating in the attack that led to Prime Minister Eduardo Dato's death. On his return to Spain in 1931, he became a Communist leader and undertook campaigns against the confederation with impunity. Another great renegade was Rafael Vidiella, who had been the editor of *Solidaridad Obrera* in 1922 and was one of the founders of the PSUC. Another leader of the Spanish Communist Party, Manuel Adame, was a CNT member who divided the organization in Andalusia and other provinces when the Republic was proclaimed. José Diáz himself, the secretary general of the Spanish Communist Party during the civil war, had been an anarchist in Andalusia.

It is well known that the CNT never took revenge upon those members who changed their political creed. The violent struggles between anarchists and communists in Seville, Malaga, Cordoba, Granada and so forth were struggles for control between rival groups, never reprisals against renegades.

The PSUC exploited the assassination of Roldán Cortada in order to add to the mounting hostility against the CNT and to set the stage for the great provocation that was soon to come. At the funeral, the PSUC organised an imposing demonstration that was 'spontaneously joined' by military forces and police, who paraded for hours down the main streets of Barcelona in a provocative manner, shouting threats against the anarchists. Cortada became the martyr, the Calvo Sotelo of the Communist crusade.

Soon threats were realised. Within a few days, Stalinists and carabinero troops from the central government clashed with the CNT militia who had been guarding the French frontier since July 19, 1936. Near Puigcerda, three CNT activists were killed in an ambush. The agitation spread to the whole frontier when confederal reinforcements arrived from Lerida, Aragon and Seo de Urgel. The incident ended only after the Barcelona CNT committees intervened and handed the town of Puigcerda over to central government troops.

And so the first of May arrived, a day traditionally celebrated in Spain in memory of the Chicago martyrs. The tension in the air spoiled any celebration of the brotherhood of the revolution. The central government, on pretext of support for fighters on the fronts and the need for war materials declared the day to be a 'day of work'. In Catalonia, the police 'worked' hard, harassing civilians with searches in the streets and other investigations. CNT members were disarmed and detained. Union cards and other confederal documents were destroyed in the presence of their holders, who were further subjected to gross indignities.

On May 2 *Solidaridad Obrera* admonished the government in the following terms:

The guarantee of the revolution is the proletariat in arms. To disarm the people is to put oneself on the other side of the barricade. No matter how much of a councillor or a commissioner one may be, one cannot order the disarming of workers who struggle against fascism with more selflessness and heroism than all the politicians of the rearguard. Workers! Let none of you be disarmed under any circumstances! That is the watchword!

This was the prelude to the great drama.

CNT poster calling on 'Telephone Workers' to defend their
interests against political intrigues and capitalism.
'Struggle to Win.'

2

The Tragic Week in May
Augustin Souchy

INTRODUCTION

On July 19th 1936, the Spanish generals rose against the people.
The workers of Barcelona, under the leadership of the anarchists,
succeeded in smashing the fascist rising within two and a half days.
The anarchists did not want to conquer power for themselves, nor
did the unions seek to establish a dictatorship. As in all other parts
of Spain, an anti-fascist united front was formed. It ranged all the
way from the various republican tendencies of the bourgeoisie to
the most extreme tendencies of the proletariat — the anarchists.
Naturally there was not complete harmony among the various
tendencies composing the anti-fascist block, either with respect to
aims or choice of means. Some wanted merely to smash the power
of the generals and the clergy, but, otherwise maintain a bourgeois
capitalist society; others sought a fundamental change in all phases
of social life. High finance was on the side of the fascist generals.
With the defeat of the generals, they lost their positions of power.
The workers' organisations assumed the functions of organising
public life. The economic transformations took the form of
socialisation. All big enterprises were either collectivised or
socialised. The former owners of these big enterprises can offer no
more resistance. However, the petty bourgeoisie, even though it
did not have the strength to resist the new developments during
the first months of proletarian victory, did not accept completely
the new order.

In the course of this development divergent trends began to
appear. The masses of the workers were for the most part
organised in the anarcho-syndicalist organisation, the CNT; the

23

petty bourgeoisie, during the months that followed the 19th of
July, affiliated itself with the UGT. Not only workers, but traders,
owners of small shops, market salesmen, etc, joined the UGT.
The developments in Spain took a course totally different from
that of other countries. Forms of organisation arose, especially in
Catalonia, which had been seen nowhere else. In all other
European countries, especially in the democratic ones, the
political parties form the currents of public life, but in Catalonia
the trade unions have this function. This is due to the syndicalist
character of the Spanish labour movement. In the spirit of these
traditions, the petty bourgeoisie also organised themselves into
trade unions.

There is a fundamental difference in the workers' organisation,
the CNT, and that of the petty bourgeoisie, the UGT — in whose
ranks workers have also been organised — both as to politics and
as to their final goal. The UGT accepted collectivisation only
under compulsion; they wanted nationalisation, that is, the power
of control to lie in the hands of the state and the political parties
represented in it rather than in the hands of the workers'organisations. Friction arose, leading to collisions. Among the workers
themselves, in the factories and in the management of enterprises,
complete understanding and harmony reigned. Only in political
questions did opinions differ.

When the CNT entered the Catalan government on September
28th 1936, after the dissolution of the Anti-fascist Militia
Committee which had been functioning for two and a half months,
it took over, officially, the Department of Food Supplies. A
central department for food supplies was created under the
direction of the syndicalist Juan Domenech. He established an
internal trade monopoly for the control of prices. The provisioning
of food for the cities was to be taken over entirely by the unions of
the transport workers and the various branches of the food
industry, who were to substitute — in accordance with a special
plan — for the big enterprise and the small traders who had
controlled the food industry until then. The small traders became
— as members of their unions — equal to the workers of town and
country. Or, rather, they were supposed to become such.
Continuous conflicts arose between the members of the CNT and
those of the UGT, over ways and means of conducting the work.
The conflicts created a scarcity of certain food articles. Things

became more expensive; sharp political discussions arose as to their cause, and as to the value of the methods.

Three months later, December 16th 1936, a new Catalan government had to be organised. This crisis was of a purely political character. The POUM, Workers Party of Marxist Union, was being viciously attacked by the leaders of the UGT, official communists for the most part. They declared the POUM, because of its Trotskyist tendency, a counter-revolutionary party. Soviet Russia herself, through her official representatives, took part in this campaign. The crisis was created in the Generality in order to remove the POUM, whose leader, Andres Nin, was Minister of Justice, from the government. The CNT was opposed to this political manoeuvre but, being in a minority in the coalition government, the POUM was expelled from the government.

The dictatorial aims of the communists manifested themselves clearly in the new order. The communists had always been an unimportant minority in Catalonia, as well as in the rest of Spain. By a series of clever manoeuvres their influence increased in Catalonia. They united with the Socialist Party of Catalonia (PSUC), which joined the 3rd International. Although they called themselves socialists, they had the support of the communist organisations, and succeeded in winning the new party over to their line. To the comunists of the PSUC the POUM signified a rival party that had to be eliminated from the scene. The Soviet Union strongly supported these manoeuvres. Some shipments of food arrived from the USSR. They also sent some armaments. The propaganda machine started using this support for their political purposes. The POUM began to lose their influence.

The influence of the PSUC grew in proportion as that of the POUM declined. The differences between the two parties were extended into the UGT. The members of the POUM belonged to the UGT and even held a number of important positions there. The PSUC wanted to expel them from their posts. A bitter conflict began between the two Marxist brothers for control of the trade unions, a conflict such as is known only too well in many other countries. The political atmosphere among the anti-fascists in Catalonia became ever more unbearable.

The CNT acted loyally toward the anti-fascist cause when the new government was formed. It wanted to stop fighting among the political parties. It made the proposal and succeeded in having it accepted, that trade unions, and not the political parties, should be represented in the new government. These trade unions were the CNT and the UGT. The Catalan Left, as a special expression of the Catalan Nation, and as partisans of the presidency, was also allowed to participate.

To get the Ministry of Defence, until then in the hands of the Catalan Left,the CNT gave up the Department of Food Supplies to the UGT. Immediately after taking over the Department, Juan Comorera, the new Minister, erased, with one stroke of his pen, the entire work of his predecessor: the inner trade monopoly, the fixed prices for articles of food, was wiped out. Comorera's aim was to break the power of the unions. He therefore wanted to turn over the function of supplying food to private companies. Thus small proprietors, petty traders and tenants were able to make greater profits through higher prices. The scarcity of bread became chronic. Things became more expensive and the masses more discontented. Economically, as well as politically, the fuel had been assembled, and demogogy helped set it alight.

On October 22nd 1936, a pact was ratified, by the CNT-FAI on one side and the UGT-PSUC on the other. They agreed to a programme of minimum demands. Both organisations, especially the CNT, made concessions in the struggle against the rebel generals. The workers rejoiced over this pact, and a great mass meeting in the vast bullring of Barcelona, where all of the city workers were assembled, sealed it by acclamation.

But there were those who still put their partisan interests above the interests of the proletariat as a whole. A campaign was begun against the CNT and the FAI of the same character as that employed against the POUM. The anarchists and syndicalists were held responsible for everything that did not function too smoothly. Even though the CNT-FAI gave up the idea of collectivisation in those sections where the small tenants were in a majority, and absolutely rejected the proposal for compulsory collectivisation, they continued to campaign against the CNT-FAI among the small tenants and peasants. They appealed to the property instinct, made the idea of collectivisation appear hostile to the lovers of property, and went so far as to denounce the advocates of collectivisation as enemies of the people.

Such a malicious campaign had its effect. In January 1937, an insurrection arranged by the politicians broke out against the CNT-FAI in the town of Fatarella. The insurrection, as such, was unimportant; but it was symptomatic. Six months had passed since the victory over the fascists, six months of revolutionary development which led, and had to lead, towards socialisation. But certain parties wanted to reverse the trend of this development. They wanted a national war, not a social revolution. The slogan 'the war and the revolution' for which the CNT-FAI stands, was opposed by the slogan of all the other political parties: 'First, we must win the war. Everything else, a new political order, establishment of social justice, etc, must be left untouched till the end of the war'.

The conflicts became more intense. They wanted to manoeuvre the CNT-FAI out of their political positions. Blood flowed in Fatarella. Although both organisations issued a joint declaration regarding the events and their origin, the PSUC press continued its campaign of slander against responsible members of the CNT-FAI, ministers in the Generality, in connection with the outbreak. Certain elements of the Catalan Left and the Catalan Nationalists (Estat Catalá) also joined in this insidious campaign.

Grave discontent reigned among the workers. The revolutionary workers of Catalonia felt humiliated by the gradual curtailment of their revolutionary conquests after the 19th of July. The representatives of the CNT-FAI vigorously opposed the application of police measures to meet the discontent of the masses. The bourgeois elements, therefore, tried to remove the advocates of the syndicalists and the anarchists from their positions. The workers' Patrols of Control, composed of those fighting elements who had smashed fascism in Catalonia on July 19th, had been functioning as anti-fascist guards, and were legalised as such. The majority of the members of these Patrols are members of the CNT, and when the UGT demanded equal representation with the CNT, to which they were obviously not entitled since they were not equal in membership in the region, bitter conflict sprang up again. The UGT members left the Patrols and devoted their attention to winning over the police to their side. Instead of building bridges of unity, they were widening the gulf that kept the proletariat separated.

The communists and the elements of the Catalan Left, the Esquerra, started an intense propaganda among the existing police bodies: Assault Guards, Civil Guards and Catalan City Guards, a propaganda directed against all syndicalists and the anarchists. The latter had been demanding from the very beginning that the old police units be dissolved and replaced by a single body for public security. The other parties and organisations opposed it. Friction arose between the police and the workers' Patrols. In some places fighting broke out resulting in a number of dead and wounded. The following is an example of the preparations being made by certain elements for a fratricidal war against the anarchists:

On Friday March 5th 1937, a few individuals presented an order, signed by Vallejo, director of the arms factories, to the arsenal in Barcelona, to hand over to them ten armoured cars. The director of the arsenal found the document in order and delivered the cars. At the last moment doubts arose as to the authenticity of the order, and the director telephoned to Vallejo for verification. The document proved to be forged, but, in the meantime the armoured cars had been driven away. They were followed and observed to go into the Voroschilov Barracks, belonging to the PSUC, that is, the communists.

Premier Tarradellas intervened. At first the barracks' officer denied all knowledge of the deed. Only when threatened with a forced investigation of the barracks did they admit that the armoured cars were there.

The purpose of thus stealing and hiding the armoured cars became more than clear to the people of Barcelona during the tragic May days.

Premier Tarradellas issued a decree prohibiting the members of the various police bodies from joining any political parties or unions, which aroused great indignation among the workers. Special plenums of the CNT were held and the representatives of the CNT in the government were instructed to demand the annulment of the decree. At the same time the workers' organisations of the CNT demanded the reform of the Department of Food Supplies and, therefore, the resignation of Comorera. A new crisis of the Generality was precipitated on March 27th.

The solution to this crisis proved to be very difficult. The demands of the PSUC, hiding behind the UGT, became ever more arrogant. When, after a week of negotiations, a new programme for the government of the Generality had been agreed upon, the UGT broke it at the very last moment. Unity, so painfully achieved, was again spoiled. Companys, president of the Catalan Generality, created a provisional government with a peaceful coup d'état. The syndicalists and anarchists would have been perfectly justified if they had rejected this arbitrary solution. They had proved their good will and patience; they could face public opinion; justice and sympathy were definately with them. Yet, not to break the anti-fascist front, they swallowed this bitter pill too. On April 16th the crisis was finally solved, the CNT proving very compliant. They renounced their former demands, modified the desires of the proletariat by pointing out the necessities of the war against fascism, and urged them to concentrate their forces for the period after the defeat of the fascists.

Comorera no longer headed the Department of Food Supplies, but the office itself remained in the hands of the UGT. The ministers of the CNT had also been changed. The syndicalists and the anarchists had done all they could to maintain the anti-fascist united front. They hoped that a new phase of development would begin now, a period of calm and relaxation behind the lines. False hopes.

On April 25th, Roldan Cortada, prominent member of the PSUC was killed near Molins de Llobregat. With this lamentable act as a pretext, the PSUC tried, through their authority over the Public Forces, to take measures of repression against the sympathizers and members of the CNT and the FAI. And although they did not accuse us directly of having committed the attentat, they nevertheless tried, through their actions, to place the moral responsibility for the criminal attentat upon our organizations. Indignation spread over the entire province of Barcelona, both for the deed, and for the harsh measures of the police. The Director of Public Security, Rodriguez Salas, was responsible for these measures. His political career had been a varied one until then. He finally landed with the UGT. His actions against the CNT were considered as provocations. He had been conducting a struggle against the CNT for several months.

A few days later the anarchist mayor of Puigcerda, Antonio Martin, and three of his comrades were shot. The members of the FAI became very indignant over the murder of their comrade, whom they all loved and respected as one of the best. Political tempers rose. The First of May was approaching. The negotiations between the CNT and the UGT for joint demonstrations failed, owing to the manoeuvres of the communists who controlled the UGT. Bitterness turned gradually into hate. Political passions dominated the scene.

THE EVENTS OF MAY 3rd

On May 3rd, Rodriguez Salas launched a new attack against the CNT. Following a preconceived plan and carrying out the orders of the Minister of the Interior, issued behind the backs of the other Councillors, he broke into the Telephone Building with a force of 200 police. This was the last straw. The avalanche finally broke loose. The patience of the workers at last was at an end. They took action against this provocation.

The Telephone Building of Barcelona is located in the centre of the city, on Plaza Catalunya. Like all public enterprises, not only in Catalonia but throughout Spain, the telephone building had been taken over by the workers' organizations and controlled by them according to the Decree of Collectivisation of October 24th, 1936. A delegate of the Catalan Generality was at the head of the control committee of the workers. This arrangement was in accord with the laws of the country. It is likely that the UGT was not satisfied with this state of affairs because it had fewer members in the control committee than the CNT. But they also had fewer members among the workers and employees of the telephone building. Rodriguez Salas, not wishing to wait until his partisans might win over a majority of the workers and employees to this organisation, decided to gain absolute control of the Telephone Exchange by force.

About three o'clock in the afternoon of May 3rd, three motor lorries of police drove up to the telephone building under his personal command. They entered the building, wanting to occupy it. The manner of their approach was, of necessity, regarded as an insulting provocation of the workers. They were asked to put up their hands and turn over their weapons. (Since last July, all responsible leaders of organisations, political parties, public institutions, etc., carry small arms. In addition, all public buildings have arms as a protection against fascists, some only rifles, and others, more important, also have machine guns.)

The workers defended themselves. A machine gun covered the police from an upper storey. They could not go beyond the first floor. While all this was taking place inside the building, word of the assault spread in the square, and soon after, throughout the city. It was as though a match had been set to gunpowder. The workers of Barcelona, belonging to the CNT in an overwhelming majority, feared that this might be only the beginning of still further actions against their rights. People came from all parts of the city to see what had happened; the police tried to keep them back; the collision had taken place.

Workers and police ran about excitedly in every section of the city. The union headquarters were full of people. Everybody wanted arms. Everybody wanted to be ready to defend other buildings from similar assaults. Perhaps, at some other time, this assault upon the telephone building might not have had such consequences. But the accumulation of political conflicts during the past few months had made the atmosphere tense. It was impossible to stem the indignation of the masses.

A few hours later, the entire city of Barcelona was in arms. The workers occupied a number of houses near Plaza Catalunga, but retired soon after. The police were concentrated near the police prefecture. The Catalan Minister of the Interior, Artemio Aiguadé, was with the police, and behind the whole section. With him were the masses of the armed Catalan Nationalists (Estat Catalá), and the militants of the PSUC. Armed troops were also concentrated in the outer districts of Barcelona. It became clear to all that they were trying to organise a putsch against the CNT and the FAI.

From the dungeons of dictatorship until today, the CNT and the FAI have always had their defence committees. These committees began to function at once, their members taking up arms.

To prevent this incident from leading to even greater collisions, the president of the police, Comrade Eroles, the general secretary of the Patrols, Comrade Asens, and Comrade Diaz, were sent as representatives of the defense committees to the Telephone Building to persuade the intruders to withdraw. the workers refused to work under the threat of the police and it was obvious that calm would not be restored until the police were removed. The effort of our three comrades came to nothing.

In the face of the increasing tension among the people of Barcelona, the Regional Committee could keep silent no longer. Its secretary, Comrade Valerio Mas, together with some other comrades, went to Premier Tarradellas and to the Minister of the Interior, Aiguadé, and asked them to remove the police in order to pacify the population. Tarradellas as well as Aiguadé assured them that they knew nothing about the incident of the Telephone

Building. But it was to be proven later that Aiguadé had himself given the order for the occupation of the Telephone Building.

The Regional Committee of the CNT announced by radio that they would do everything possible to compel the police to withdraw from the building. The workers were asked to maintain their calm and dignity. In the course of the negotiations, the government promised to order the withdrawal of the police. The armed workers also retreated. For the time being everything seemed to be normal again. But soon the news began to spread that Salas' police were disarming the workers, and once again the masses became anxious.

The workers were on their guard. They did not trust the apparent peace and remained in watchful positions. In the meantime blood had already been shed. The shooting had begun and two people were wounded.

Among the people the nervous tension continued. The workers demanded guarantees. They did not want any repetitions of such incidents. They demanded, through their organisation, the dismissal of the Secretary of Public Security, Salas, and of the Minister of the Interior, Aiguadé. If these demands were not fulfilled, they would declare a general strike. Their resignations were not announced.

On the following day, a general strike was declared. Had the other parties agreed to the dismissal of these two men, calm would have been restored and the terrible tragedy avoided. Negotiations were carried on till 6 o'clock in the morning — fruitlessly. Toward morning the workers began building barricades in the outer districts of the city. There was no fighting during this first night, but the general tension increased. In some parts of the city shots were being fired. In the district of Sarria some hundred workers armed themselves, built a barricade, and disarmed the civil guards, who consented to such a course. There was no bloodshed there. The workers were masters of the situation.

In the district of Sans, where Durruti lived for many years, the workers, especially the Libertarian Youth, assembled in their cultural centres (Ateneos) and built barricades...No fighting...In the district of Hostafranchs the workers built barricades during the night of May 3rd-4th. The civil guards were disarmed by the workers without offering resistance. The large bullring, situated in this district, was also occupied by militiamen on leave from

Barcelona. In the Lerida streets, 300 civil guards handed their arms to the workers.

No fighting took place in the outer districts of the city, partly because the police were on the side of the workers, and partly because the workers were in such an absolute majority that resistance seemed futile.

TUESDAY, MAY 4th

During the early hours of the morning the shooting started in the centre of the city. The Palace of Justice was occupied by the police. Fighting centres sprang up everywhere. A few headquarters of the CNT were seized by the police. By eleven o'clock in the morning the delegates of the CNT unions were holding a special meeting where they agreed to do everything possible to re-establish calm. A special committee was elected to negotiate with the government for a solution to the conflict. The CNT issued an appeal to the police, declaring:

"It is necessary to come to a speedy solution to this conflict. The incidents now taking place in the street are the result of a long and painful development to sacrifice the organisation of the CNT and its leaders after using their blood and their strength to defeat the treacherous fascists. Don't let them betray you! You know very well, and you have the proof of it, that the CNT-FAI are not against you, either as individuals or collectively. You are, like ourselves, soldiers of the anti-fascist front. Offer your arms to the people and place yourselves on their side as you did on the 19th of July. Neither the CNT nor the FAI want to establish a dictatorship. Nor will they ever tolerate dictatorship so long as a single one of their members is alive. We do not fight against fascism out of love for war; we are fighting to secure public freedom and to prevent the massacre and the exploitation of the people by those, who, without calling themselves fascists, nevertheless want to establish a regime of absolutism, in complete violation of the feelings and the traditions of our people."

One hour later the Regional Committees of the CNT and the FAI spoke to the people of Barcelona:

"The CNT and the FAI address you now to tell you that they do not want to shed the blood of fellow workers in the streets of

Barcelona. But we cannot endure the provocations of those, who, misusing their public offices, want to destroy the rights of the workers of the CNT and the UGT, as was the case yesterday when they tried to occupy the Telephone Building by force of arms."

Soon after, another manifesto of the CNT was broadcast to the workers of Barcelona:

"Men and women of the people! Workers! We speak frankly to the public, which, as always in the past, is proof of our honesty. We are not responsible for what is now taking place. We are not attacking. We are only defending ourselves. We did not start this; we did not provoke it. We are merely answering the abuse, the calumny, and the force that has been directed against the CNT and the FAI, the most implacable antifascists of all.

"We have never concealed our aims; we have given ample proof of our worth. Why do they want to eliminate us? Does it not seem suspicious to you that they are attacking the CNT and the FAI, while in Madrid, in Andalusia, in Viscaya, and in Aragon our forces have given, and are still giving at the present time, proof of the utmost courage and strength? Workers of the CNT and the UGT! Remember the road we have travelled together. How many have fallen, covered in blood, in the open streets and on the barricades! Put down your weapons! Embrace as brothers! We shall be victorious if we are united. If we fight amongst ourselves, we must go down to defeat. Consider! We extend our hand without weapons. You do the same and everything will be forgotten.

"Unity among ourselves! Death to fascism!"

One hour later, at 3 o'clock in the afternoon, the CNT and the FAI again broadcast a message to the people of Barcelona:

"The CNT and the FAI, who helped decisively in the defeat of fascism in Barcelona and Catalonia alongside the other antifascist organisations, appeal to you to-day, to all of you, to put down your arms. Think of our great goal, common to all the workers, in the rear and at the front.

"The government of the Generality must be cleaned out. These demoralising acts will have to cease regardless of who is performing them, including the ministers.

"Workers of the CNT! Workers of the UGT! Don't be deceived by these manoeuvres. Above all else, Unity! Put down your arms. Only one slogan: We must work to beat fascism! Down with fascism!"

Despite all these appeals and demonstrations of good-will to the police and the population of Barcelona, the hostilities, once started, were not to be held back. Indignation and bitterness increased on all sides. Four ministers of the CNT, who were in their respective offices when the hostilities broke out, could not reach the seat of the Generality — and no longer wanted to. The ministers of the other parties, especially the Premier, Tarradellas, and President Companys, declared that they could not carry on negotiations so long as the streets were not cleared of the armed forces, yet it was obvious to all that the continued presence of the armed forces in the streets was not due to the anarchists and syndicalists, but to the undisciplined police under the command of provacateur agents of the PSUC and the Estat Catalá. The responsible organs of the CNT and the FAI had given ample proof of their desire to end the conflict by their manifestos to the people. The prolongation of the negotiations were, of necessity, fatal. The bitterness and the hatred grew by the hour. An explosion, a violent bloody fratricidal war might break out at any moment. The Catalan city police, and the members of the PSUC working with them, opened the hostilities in the centre of the city.

At about 5 o'clock in the afternoon, an exceptionally cruel and bloody incident occurred on Via Durruti, not far from Casa CNT-FAI headquarters of the Regional Committees of the two organisations. Two cars were coming up the street from the direction of the docks to get to the Regional Committee. Some 300 metres from the Casa, a barricàde of Catalan city guards and members of the PSUC, with red arm-bands was located. As the cars approached this barricade, they were ordered to stop and surrender their weapons. As they were getting out of the car to carry out the order, they were shot down by volleys of rifle fire.

This incident, witnessed by many from the windows of the Casa CNT-FAI, aroused fierce indignation. The defenders of the Casa wanted to avenge the cowardly murder immediately. But after discussion decided to allow even this provocation to go unanswered, so as to avoid still greater harm.

As it became apparent that the police not only did not intend to stop the hostilities, but were actually preparing to attack the headquarters of the Regional Committee itself, the Defence Committee decided to order two armoured cars from the arms factories for the defence of the Casa and its inmates. They arrived during the evening, and for the duration of hostilities, were held ready for defence.

In the meantime, a sort of united front had been established between the Catalan Left (Esquerra), the Catalan Nationalists (Estat Catalá), and the PSUC and UGT. They all defended the Minister of the Interior, Aiguadé, and the Chief of Police, Rodriguez Salas, the two most directly responsible for the outbreak. This united front among the Ministers was carried into the street. Police, national Guards, Catalan city police, and members of the PSUC (affiliated to the 3rd International) and the UGT manned the barricades together against the workers of the CNT and the FAI, with whom the POUM, the Party of Marxist Unity, were also allied. This united front of all the left bourgeois parties with the communists against the syndicalist CNT and the anarchist FAI was ample proof that they were trying to create a situation in which they could remove the syndicalists and the anarchists from the government and discredit them among the workers. Although all the leaders of these parties may not have participated in the preparation of the conflict, it was, nevertheless, undeniable that all of them did not want to take advantage of it to remove, or at least weaken, the influence of that part of the Catalan proletariat that considers the struggle against fascism a simultaneous struggle against capitalism and for socialism. What had been carried out some months ago against the smaller party of the POUM with comparatively little effort was to be continued now against the mass organisations of the Catalan proletariat by the use of force. That the police under Rodriguez Salas had rebelled against the government was never stated in the official reports of the government. The population had to be told that the workers of the CNT and the FAI had initiated the conflict.

Not only the Regional Committee of the CNT and FAI, and the assemblies of their delegates; not only the representatives of the various districts of the city, who were at the head of their barricades, favoured a peaceful solution of the conflict. The National Committee of CNT and its representatives in Valencia also demanded it. Shortly after 5 o'clock in the afternoon a delegation arrived from Valencia, consisting of the secretary of the National Committee of the CNT, Mariano Vasquez, and the

Minister of Justice, Garcia Oliver, a well known anarchist.
Members of the Executive Committee of the UGT also came from
Valencia. Federica Montseny, Minister of Public Health, also
came to Barcelona. At a joint conference, it was decided in accord
with a proposal from the CNT to issue an appeal to the people to
stop the hostilities and lay down their arms. This plan was
discussed for two hours, the PSUC delegates displaying the
greatest opposition. Sancajo, representing the Executive Committee of the UGT, Mariano Vasquez, as secretary of the CNT,
Garcia Oliver, the anarchist Minister, and President Companys,
all spoke over the radio calling upon the people of Barcelona to
stop the fighting.

The secretary of the National Committee, Mariano Vasquez,
speaking over the Generality radio station said:

"We must stop what is happening immediately. We must stop
immediately so that our comrades at the front may see that we
fully understand the present situation, so that they can face the
enemy secure in the knowledge that they do not have to watch the
rear because we cannot reach an agreement. Let us keep the
present situation in mind! We must not suffer for another moment
that feeling of collapse in the rear, which can only give comfort to
fascism. Stop the shooting, comrades! But let no one try to
conquer new positions when the firing has stopped.

"We shall continue our discussions here until we have found a
solution. The demands of self-preservation drive us to the unity of
all the anti-fascist organisations of Catalonia. We are all assembled
here, especially the Executive Committee of the UGT and the
National Committee of the CNT who have come from Valencia to
end this terrible conflict in Barcelona. We have come together to
seek a joint agreement because this fighting can only serve the
purposes of our enemy — fascism!"

The negotiations in the Palace of the Generality continued
during the entire night. Although the members of the syndicalist
trade unions and of the Anarchist Federation of Iberia obeyed the
appeal to stop hostilities, the rebel police, and even worse the
members of other hostile parties, continued their criminal
activities. During that very night the CNT Union of Hide and
Leather workers were attacked in their headquarters. During the
entire night intense rifle fire could be heard in the centre of the
city.

WEDNESDAY, MAY 5th

The night-long negotiations resulted in the resignation of the
entire government. A provisional government was formed of one
representative from each party that was represented in the former
government. But calm was not restored. Upon the return of the
representatives of the CNT-FAI from the Generality, the various
committees of the CNT-FAI held a meeting. The two officials
involved (Aiguadé and Salas) whose dismissal was demanded by
the workers, resigned with the rest of the Council of the
Generality, and steps were taken to assure their continued absence
from such responsible posts. When reports came in from Coll
Blanch that further clashes were feared, the Committee of the
CNT and the FAI took steps to call upon the workers to desist
from their efforts to occupy the barracks. Again the workers did
everything possible to avoid conflict.

At 9.30 in the morning the assault guards offered a new
provocation. They attacked the headquarters of the Medical
Union at Santa Ana Square in the centre of the city. At the same
time they attacked, with greater fury, the headquarters of the
Local Federation of the Libertarian Youth. The youth defended
themselves heroically. Six young anarchists were killed in the
defence of their premises. Both places telephoned the Regional
Committee for help. The rifle fire, explosions of hand grenades
and machine gun fire could be clearly heard throughout the centre
of the city. The streets in the fighting zone were deserted; no one
dared to go out.

When, in the afternoon, the hostilities still continued the
Defence Committee decided to call for three more armoured cars
to defend the threatened Union headquarters. They came within a
few hours to the Casa CNT-FAI, and were put into action to aid
and support endangered unions and comrades. Soon after their
arrival the tanks had a chance to go into action. Opposite the
Regional Committee, three unarmed workers were being shot at
in the street. The shooting came from the barricades of the PSUC
mentioned before. The unarmed workers were seeking refuge in a
doorway. They seemed lost. One of the armoured cars went to the
rescue of the endangered comrades upon the intitiative of a
woman comrade.

Wild rumours were spreading through the city. Uncontrolled

elements — they said — want to continue the Revolution. This was the third day of struggle and there seemed to be no hope for the re-establishment of peace. The Generality radio station spoke of the uncontrolled elements of the CNT and the FAI. The Regional Committee asked the Generality over the telephone who was controlling the police. For, although we were assured again and again that the police would not shoot any more, machine gun and rifle fire continued to be heard coming from those sections of the city where the police had their strongholds. At five in the afternoon the Regional Committee of the CNT proposed the following:

Hostilities to cease.

Every party to keep its positions.

The police and civilians fighting on their side be specifically asked to stop fighting.

The responsible committees to be informed at once if the pact is broken anywhere.

Solitary shots should not be answered.

The defenders of the Union quarters to remain passive and await further instructions.

During the fighting between the Catalan city guards and the assault guards against the Libertarian Youth, an assault guard was taken prisoner, but set free soon after to have his slight wound treated professionally.

The proposals for armistice were accepted by the government, but the armed forces supposedly acting in defence of said government, paid no attention to it. During the afternoon they tried to encircle the headquarters of the Regional Committee, the Casa CNT-FAI. The rebels built new barricades, closer to the Regional Committee. The shooting never stopped.

Rumours of the events in Barcelona reached the front. The well-known anarchist, Jover, rushed from Huesca to Barcelona. The militia at the front were concerned over the fate of Barcelona; they did not want it to fall into the hands of these counter-revolutionaries in disguise. It had become obvious that the Catalan city guards and the assault guards, who were both being manipulated by agent provocateurs, and part of the petty bourgeoisie, seemed to be on the side of the anti-fascist coalition government. Actually they were pursuing different aims. All these elements were by now uncontrolled by the government. They had become a horde of counter-revolutionists set loose against the proletariat, and, specifically, against its organisations, the CNT and the FAI. In the face of the growing danger for the workers, for their union headquarters, their cultural centres and, above all, for the lives of all the militants, it was decided to organise a stronger defence. A Regional Defence Committee was created. Their deliberations in the Regional Committee were punctuated by continuous machine gun fire. Thus, the defence of the Casa CNT-FAI was organised. Reports came in from all parts of Barcelona and from the provinces of Catalonia that the overwhelming majority of the population were with the CNT, and that most towns and villages were in the hands of our organisations. It would have been easy to attack the centre of the city had the responsible committees so decided. They only had to appeal to the defence committees of the outlying districts. But the Regional Committee of the CNT was opposed to it. Every proposal of attack was unanimously rejected by them and by the FAI.

A newly founded group, called 'Friends of Durruti' functioning on the fringes of the CNT-FAI, published a proclamation declaring that, "A revolutionary Junta has been constituted in Barcelona. All those responsible for the putsch, manoeuvring under the protection of the government, shall be executed. The POUM shall be a member of the Revolutionary Junta because they stood by the workers."

The Regional Committees decided not to concur with this proclamation. The Libertarian Youth likewise rejected it. On the next day, Thursday May 6th, their official statement was printed in the entire press of Barcelona.

THE MURDER OF BERNERI AND BARBIERI

There was fighting during the following night. But an incident occurred in the evening that demonstrated clearly the intentions of the provocateurs. A short way down the Via Durruti, opposite the Regional Committee at 2 Plaza del Angel, lived the well known anarchist militant, Camillo Berneri. A number of other Italian exiles, who had come to Spain to form an anti-fascist column, also lived there. Berneri was a sort of political delegate among his countrymen. He also edited the Italian paper *Guerra di Classe*, in which he drew attention to the dangers of dictatorship. One article entitled 'Burgos and Moscow', attracted the attention of the Russian government. Berneri wrote:

"Once fascism is beaten, it will be necessary for the CNT and the FAI to continue the struggle for their social programme. The Executive Committee of the Communist Party of Spain declared only the other day that, in the present struggle in Spain, they are defending democracy and private property. It smells of Noske. Were not Madrid in flames one might even expect a new Kronstadt. But Madrid is approaching victory. Revolutionary Catalonia receives neither arms nor financial help. Did the USSR send arms, munitions, and military cadres in order to control the anti-fascist fight and check the development of the Social Revolution? The alternative, Madrid or Franco, has paralysed Spanish anarchism. Today Barcelona is located between Burgos, Rome, Madrid, and Moscow. It is besieged. The horizon is hazy. We are on the high seas in a great storm. Shall we be able to perform wonders? Crushed between the Prussians and Versailles, the Commune of Paris initiated a fire that lit up the world. Between Burgos and Madrid lies Barcelona. Let the Godets of Moscow remember this." [Godet was the fascist general who led the uprising in Barcelona on the 19th of July. He was duly tried by the people of Barcelona, and shot.]

This article caused Russia to intervene in the CNT-FAI. Since then, Berneri was anathema to the partisans of the Communist Party Dictatorship.

When the hostilities started, Berneri was in his rooms with his friend, Barbieri, also a well known anarchist. With them were the wife of Barbieri and Tosca Pantini, widow of an Italian militiaman killed on the Aragon front. The Italians' house was surrounded by Catalan city guards and members of the PSUC wearing red armbands with their party insignia on them. On the morning of Tuesday May 4th, the Catalan and Communist guards came to the house and told the Italian anarchists to be careful because there was a lot of shooting in the neighbourhood. There was another visit in the afternoon for the purpose of registering the house and conficating the arms which belonged to Italian militiamen on leave in Barcelona. The next day, Wednesday May 5th, at about 5 o'clock in the afternoon, Berneri and Barbieri were taken away by 12 guards, six of them from the city police, the others were members of the PSUC as evidenced by their red armbands. The leader of the group, showing his badge with the number 1109, asked for their names. Two of the group remained in the house to carry out a further search. Berneri had been working on a book about Mussolini's policy in the Mediterranean, with special reference to the Balearic Islands. It was a book against Italian fascism.

Barbieri's wife wanted to go with the two comrades when they were taken away, but they refused to allow her.

Both men were shot during the following night, by machine gun fire, as revealed by the autopsy. It was cold blooded murder, since both men were unarmed. The murder was committed near the Palace of the Generality. Soon after the bodies of the two anarchists were delivered to the mortuary of the Hospital Clinico. The lists show that the Red Cross had found both bodies near the Generality.

The evidence is irrefutable. Berneri and Barbieri were shot because they were anarchists by police and members of the PSUC, i.e. faithful Moscow Communists. Barbieri's companion declared: "Barbieri asked why they who were anarchists and therefore anti-fascists, were being ill treated. And the leader of the group answered: 'It's because you are anarchists that you are counter-revolutionaries.'"

The anarchists were persecuted; the anarchists were murdered; the anarchists were outlawed. Still they limited themselves only to defence, and never attacked. Yet when the lie was circulated that the anarchists were doing the attacking, the world press seized upon it eagerly and spread it to the four corners of the earth.

On the following day the papers published the number of victims: 500 dead and over 1500 wounded. A terrible indictment of those who had provoked such a fratricidal war.

THURSDAY, MAY 6th

During the night the two trade unions, the UGT and the CNT, agreed to call upon the workers once more to return to work. They published the following manifesto:

"The tragic events taking place in our city during the last 48 hours have made it impossible for the workers to go to work. The anti-fascist organisations and parties in session at the Palace of the Generality have solved the conflict that has created this abnormal situation, so harmful to the cause of the proletariat. The local federations of the CNT and the UGT have agreed to ask all members to resume their work as usual. It is necessary to return to normal life. To continue the present inactivity in the factories at this time is to weaken our forces and strengthen that of our common enemy.

"Accordingly, all workers of the CNT and the UGT are ordered to return to work. All members of both trade unions should avoid anything that might lead to possible friction and disturbances at their place of work. These events have taught us that from now on we shall have to establish relations of cordiality and comradeship, the lack of which we have all regretted deeply during the last few days.

"The local federations of the UGT and the CNT urge their members to refrain from all manifestations of hostility. Mutual understanding and solidarity are the requirements of the hour. The union cards of both organisations must be respected by everyone, and it is the duty of the control committees to respect all workers without exception.

"To work, comrades of the CNT and UGT!"

Local Federation of the CNT, Barcelona.
Local Federation of the UGT, Barcelona.

This appeal was broadcast over the radio and appeared the next morning in every paper in Barcelona. But to no avail. Work was not resumed anywhere. The police continued in their hostile attitude and fortified their positions further during the night with the obvious intention of extending the struggle. Provocations by the political parties continued in the hope of shaking the faith of the workers in the conduct of the committees of the CNT and the FAI. The fighting was resumed. Bitterness and discontent filled the workers. The Valencia government intervened more energetically into the affairs of Barcelona. Two Spanish warships were ordered to the port of Barcelona.

The streets presented a calmer picture on Thursday morning. The centre of the old city was still like a fortress. Some horse carts were already making their appearance on the wider streets, and an occasional pedestrian could be seen. The overhead wires of the tramways were being repaired. The Valencia government, it was rumoured, was gathering troops from different sectors of the front to be sent to Catalonia.

The Regional Committee and the syndicates all over the city suffered new anxieties when the police and the civilian fighters of PSUC proceeded to take advantage of the armistice to build new fortifications. Thus, the police openly carried sand bags and machine guns up to the towers of a cathedral not two hundred metres from the Casa CNT-FAI. This hardly looked like peace. Those who seek peace don't proceed to occupy new offensive positions.

Further news added to the anxiety. 1,500 troops are on their way from Valencia. Another 2,500 will follow. Against whom are they mobilising? Against the workers? In the streets of Barcelona everybody was being searched. Those who had membership *carnets* from the CNT were regarded as enemies. The *carnet* was taken away and torn up. Often, mere possession of such a document was cause for arrest. Dozens of such arrests were being made.

The negotiations between the antagonistic parties were delayed half a day by the death of the secretary of the UGT of Catalonia, Antonio Sesé. He was fatally wounded by a bullet on his way to the Generality in his own car. The shot came from the direction of the Paseo de Gracia, where his own party comrades had a barricade. The comrades who accompanied Sesé signed a document stating the facts of the case, which is now in the hands of the Theatre Union in front of whose headquarters the accident occurred. Sesé was neither murdered nor executed. Yet his death was used to intensify the insidious campaign against the CNT.

A strange situation had developed inside the Telephone Building. The workers in the upper storeys and the assault guards arranged an armistice. They allowed the workers to receive food — the first since Monday. The discussions among the workers who belonged both to the CNT and the UGT, still continued. To end these discussions and to show their willingness to restore peace, the members of the CNT agreed to leave the building at 3 o'clock in the afternoon. The assault guards were supposed to leave also. However, instead of leaving that part of the building which they had occupied earlier in the week, the assault guards proceeded to occupy the entire building, *and brought in members of the UGT to take over the posts of CNT workers*. The members of the CNT saw that they had been betrayed and immediately informed the Regional Committee. The latter intervened with the Government. They demanded that the police be withdrawn from the building. To remain meant a broken promise would render their agreements valueless for the future. Those who broke their agreement would have to take the consequences. Half an hour later the Generality replied: the *fait accompli* cannot be recalled.

This broken agreement aroused great indignation among the workers of the CNT. Had the workers in the outlying districts been informed immediately of this development, they would surely have insisted upon taking firmer measures and returned to the attack. But when the matter was discussed later, the more moderate point of view won out.

It was obvious that the occupation of the Telephone Building would be used to facilitate new attacks. And within the hour, at about 4pm, a new attack was launched against the main railroad station, Estacion de Francia. The assault guards attacked from one side; the PSUC from the Karl Marx Barracks on the other. The workers could no longer depend on the telephone. The atmosphere in the centre of the city became tense. Bombs exploded. Rifle and machine gun fire broke the silence of the metropolis.

At ten minutes past four, the Under Secretary of State, Juanel Molina, member of the FAI, communicated that General Pozas had presented himself at the Capitania to take over his office as Chief of the Fourth Brigade of the Spanish Army. The post of Catalan Minister of Defence had ceased to exist. Under Secretary of State Juanel Molina, even though he was a member of the FAI, did everything to keep the troops from entering the struggle. Had the FAI really gone into action, the entire military force would have been on their side and victory would have been certain. But the FAI did not want a fratricidal war within the ranks of the anti-fascists.

Not only at the station, but also in the neighbourhood of Plaza de Catalunya, the police started attacking the workers. In both cases the attacks were successfully repelled. Again the workers refused to counter-attack. Still, they were determined to defend their positions, their lives and their rights.

The Regional Committee was informed that the armed forces of the Catalan Nationalists and the PSUC had taken possession of the village of San Juan. The armed workers of the CNT and the FAI entered the village, disarmed the enemy and liberated their comrades. In the open village square they had to answer for their actions. They were warned not to take up arms against the people. Then the anarchists set their enemies free again.

We must mention these incidents to counteract the calumnies spread against the anarchists and the anarcho-syndicalists of Catalonia, whom they characterise as murderers and criminals.

At six o'clock they telephoned that 1,500 Assault Guards had reached Tortosa on their way to Barcelona. They occupied the headquarters of the CNT unions, the cultural centres of the FAI and the Anarchist Youth, arresting all those found inside. These troops had come from the central part of Spain. According to the evening paper *Noticiero Universal* of Saturday May 8th, these troops had come from the trenches of the Jarama front, where they had been fighting for four months alongside the International Brigade. The anarchists could also have called in their columns from the Aragon front, as well as armed forces from other parts of Catalonia, and there is no doubt that they could have been victorious within 24 hours. But they did not want to break up the anti-fascist front. They never did more than defend themselves against the attacks directed against them.

At 6.45 the united committees of the CNT and the FAI sent a new delegation to the government to find out what they intended doing. A few minutes later, news came from London by cable that the British Government had sent a torpedo boat and a cruiser, the 'Despatch', to Catalan waters near Barcelona. A delegation of CNT workers arrived to find out what the responsible committees were going to do. The committees decided to address the population of Barcelona by manifesto that they wished to maintain the anti-fascist front. At the same time they addressed the general public all over the world by a manifesto on Thursday May 6th, which reads as follows:

"While the tragic events were taking place here in Barcelona, provoked as they were by some irresponsible elements in the anti-fascist organisations, the world at large received very little information concerning the whole situation.

"The same cowardly elements that wished to provoke bloodshed in Barcelona, issued false reports to the outside world with the same evil intentions, grossly misrepresenting everything.

"Foreign countries have been told that the CNT and the FAI

were the cause of the disturbances of the last few days. You were told that the anarchists were guilty of starting this struggle among fellow workers which caused blood to flow in the streets of Barcelona. You were told that the anarchists attacked the police, the Generality, and other municipal and state institutions.

"Nothing is more false than this version of the developments and those who spread such lies intentionally can be nothing but fascists in disguise.

"Now that we have returned to normal, and those responsible for the outbreak have been dismissed from public office, when all the workers have returned to their jobs, and Barcelona is once more calm, the CNT and the FAI want to give an exact explanation of what happened.

"We are authorised to state that neither the National Confederation of Labour, nor the Iberian Anarchist Federation, or any of its dependent organisations, broke, or had any intention of breaking the anti-fascist front. The CNT and the FAI continue to collaborate loyally as in the past, with all political and trade union sectors of the anti-fascist front. The best proof of this is that the CNT continues to collaborate with the central Government, the Government of the Generality and all the municipalities.

"When the conflict started in Barcelona, the Regional and National organisations of the CNT offered every means to the government to help solve the conflict as quickly as possible. On the second day of the struggle, the secretary of the National Committee of the CNT, and the Minister of Justice, also a member of the CNT, came to Barcelona and did everything humanly possible to end this fratricidal struggle. In addition to these attempts to deal with responsible members of the other political sectors, these comrades spoke to the population of Barcelona, and called upon them to be calm and work for an agreement, and appealed for unity of action against the common enemy, fascism.

"Not only the National Committee, but also the Regional Committee, did everything possible to find a solution to this conflict. The press of the CNT of Catalonia appealed for calm and called upon the population to return to work. The news issued by radio to the unions and to the defence committees were nothing but appeals for calm.

"Further proof that the CNT did not want to break, and did not break, the anti-fascist front, is that when the new government of the Generality was formed, on the 5th of May, the representatives

of the CNT of Catalonia offered it every facility, and the secretary
of the CNT was a member of the Government.

"We are also authorised to state that neither the National
Confederation of Labour nor the Iberian Anarchist Federation
attacked any police headquarters or any other institutions of the
State or the Generality. At no time and at no place did the first
shot ever come from any responsible members of the CNT.

"The members of the CNT who controlled the Defence Council
of the Generality gave orders to all their forces not to intervene on
either side in the conflict. And they also saw to it that their orders
were obeyed.

"The Defence Committee of the CNT also gave orders to every
district of Barcelona that no one should come from there to the
centre to answer the provocations. These orders, too, were carried
out because no one actually did come to the centre to answer the
provocations.

"The Regional Committee of the CNT and the FAI gave precise
orders that no one should move from his section, that no one
should disturb the public order.

"The CNT and the FAI not only merely maintained positions of
defence, they did everything possible to try to re-establish public
order and unmask the provocateurs. Many were the traps laid for
the CNT up to the very end, but the CNT remained firm in its
position and did not allow itself to be provoked. It did not fall into
the net, which had many ramifications in the regional, national
and international spheres. And in maintaining its positions, it did
everything possible to have the provocateurs, Rodriguez Salas and
Aiguadé, removed from their responsible positions. Once this was
accomplished, and calm re-established, the CNT and the UGT,
together with the other anti-fascist forces, formed a commission to
clarify the events in Barcelona and re-establish a normal
atmosphere.

"When the causes of the disturbances were discovered, the
people returned to work. Everybody, with utmost courage and
energy, is now dedicating all their strength to the fight against
fascism, because it is the only enemy of all the workers in
Catalonia.

"The workers of Catalonia have returned to work under the
following slogans: 'No more provocateurs in the rear!' 'Unity
between the CNT and the UGT'! 'Death to fascism!'"

Meanwhile sporadic collisions and exchanges of shots continued in various sectors of the city. At about 10pm the CNT-FAI made new proposals to cease hostilities as follows: All parties and groups obligated to remove their armed guards and Patrols from the barricades. All prisoners from both sides are to be released immediately. No reprisals shall be taken. An answer was required within two hours.

At midnight the government had not sent its answer. Meanwhile disturbing news came through from Tarragona and Reus, where members of the PSUC and the Estat Catalá, taking advantage of the presence of some assault guards passing through on their way to Barcelona, used their temporary advantage to disarm and kill the workers. Telephone calls caused great anxiety. Steps were taken to counteract the news and any possible false rumours that might be coming through the telephone exchange. Important news could no longer be communicated by telephone. The radio station of the CNT was used to inform members of the organisation.

The CNT tried to extract a promise from the government in Valencia and Barcelona that the assault guards would not enter the city immediately, but should be held outside the city limits until the situation had cleared up. The arrival of the troops while the people were still so tense, would undoubtedly mean a renewal of hostilities and further loss of lives. The CNT and the FAI wanted to avoid this. They were somewhat sceptical regarding the assurances that the troops would be loyal to the workers.

The night of May 6-7th was decisive for the immediate future. The CNT and the FAI had not yet exerted the full pressure of their strength. They still continued in a waiting position. Should they summon all of Catalonia to take up the fight against the nationalists and the provocateur elements among the police and some of their chiefs? They could have rallied a tremendous force but they did not want to continue this fratricidal conflict. Again and again the anarchists offered to negotiate, eager to end the conflict. But the atmosphere was tense and the situation continued to be difficult. Fighting was going on in Tortosa and in Tarragona. At twenty past one, new telephone calls to the representatives of the government. No satisfactory answer to their proposals. The assault guards were continuing their march on Barcelona. In the centre of the city, the Catalan Nationalists and the rebellious police kept coming closer and closer to the headquarters of the Regional Committee. In San Pedro street in the immediate vicinity of the building, a new barricade was erected by the police. They were trying to encircle the Regional Committee of the CNT and the FAI.

At two in the morning the government had still failed to answer the proposals, awaited with so much impatience and anxiety... Twenty minutes past two. No answer... Half past two. No answer... A quarter to three... Three o'clock. Still no answer. They were discussing the resumption of work in the outlying districts where the fighting had stopped. The traffic could not start unless the barricades were pulled down. The delegates of the transport workers union were awaiting the answer of the government in order to give the order to start work again... A quarter to four and still no answer... At five minutes to four in the morning, the Provincial Committee communicated that they were ready to hold up the troops from Valencia... Four o'clock. No answer.

At last, at a quarter past five, the government answered. They agreed to the armistice. All parties shall leave the barricades. Patrols and guards retire to their headquarters, unions and fortified positions. Both sides to release their prisoners. The patrols to resume their functions.

Everybody relaxed. But — could one trust the sincerity of this answer? Would the workers in the telephone exchange continue to function as before? Would everything come out all right again?

Neither victors nor vanquished. That is the will of the syndicalists and anarchists. The anti-fascist front shall not be destroyed. War against fascism. Unity of all workers. That is the firm wish of the workers on the barricades. And the resolutions of the committees were based on this wish. The Regional Committee issued the following statement over the radio:

"To all the workers of the CNT: Having reached an understanding with both the political and the trade union representatives, we wish to notify you that you will receive instructions from your responsible committees regarding the establishment of complete peace and calm. For the present we urge you to keep that calm and presence of mind that the situation requires. Do not answer the provocations of those who seek to perpetuate the existing state of disorder."

While the results were still being discussed, new fears arose as the shooting broke out again to disturb the enveloping silence of the night. Two cars were driving down Via Durruti. As they passed the police prefecture, they were shot at. They were able to pass the headquarters of the Regional Committee undisturbed, but a short distance away the shooting broke out in full force once more. Rifles, machine guns, hand grenades came into play. A bad sign. A strange contrast to the assurances of a peaceful solution of the conflict. Only half an hour to 6 o'clock. Will we be able to pacify the suspicions and the tempers of the comrades? At six o'clock, shots could still be heard.

We switched off the lights. A beautiful morning. Barcelona slept in silence.

FRIDAY, MAY 7th

A few hours later, Barcelona had undergone an almost complete change. True to their agreement, the workers had left the barricades. In many places the barricades had already been torn down. They had withdrawn from the buildings. But they were keeping their arms.

In the centre of the city, however, the air was still tense. The barricades of the assault guards, of the Catalan Nationalists, and of the PSUC remained intact. And guarded. Taking advantage of the good will of the workers, groups of assault guards were walking about disarming workers wherever they could get hold of them. New friction arose between the assault guards and the Libertarian Youth in the Plaza del Pino and the Puertafer. And once more it was thanks to the initiative of the Anarchist Youth, who went unarmed to the headquarters of the assault guards to negotiate, that finally, after hours of discussion, the assault guards decided to show a more peaceful attitude and the barricades could come down.

The centre of the city was like a fortress. High buildings had been used as fortifications by the various groups. Out of walls of sand bags, mattresses or cushions, rifles and machine guns poked their barrels. The assault guards had opened the churches and used them as fortifications.

But the populace could breathe more freely. For three days they had been forced to remain in their houses. Now everybody was walking about in the streets. The masses of people pushed their way through the barricades. Children played at revolution, rolling up a rock in a piece of paper and throwing it at the counter-revolutionists from behind the barricades. Everybody was discussing the situation in the bars and cafes.

Around midday another incident occurred. In the Calle Boqueria, a car of the Libertarian Youth was stopped by an assault guard, the youth disarmed and arrested. This was an obvious breaking of the agreement that there should be no more arrests and no more reprisals. In the calle San Pedro, CNT people were also threatened by the assault guards. Towards evening further incidents occurred. Near the Arco de Triumfo and in the Puerta del Angel shots were fired, not by the workers of the CNT but by the rebellious police. The car of Federica Montseny, Minister of Public Health, was also shot at, one of the passengers being wounded.

At twenty past eight the assault guards from Valencia reached Barcelona. They drove down the Via Durruti in motor trucks, and were welcomed at the Police Prefecture. What will their attitude be towards the workers? And what attitude will the workers take? As they passed the headquarters of the Regional Committee, a shot was fired from one car, while from another came the cry, "Viva la FAI". Obviously their feelings and attitude toward the workers, toward the syndicalists and anarchists of Catalonia, were as mixed as their composition.

The workers had put down their arms and they did not think of taking them up again. The conflict was over. The workers were true to their agreement. But the other side did not prove as honourable in upholding their part of the bargain. However, everything remained quiet. No matter how much they tried to provoke the workers of the CNT and the FAI, the latter kept their presence of mind and their dignity. The workers of the CNT and the FAI had not started this conflict, nor did they want any part in prolonging it. They had not been conquered, even though the Catalan police assumed a provocatively boastful attitude after the Valencia troops arrived. Again and again they tried to put the workers in the position of the defeated party.

Yet their own conduct had been strange. The Catalan nationalists, always strongly opposed to the influence of Madrid and fighting strenuously for autonomy, had appealed for help to the Valencia Government to defend their privileges. They played the same role now as the Catalan Right parties had played a few years before. In October 1934, Cambó and his League insisted on the intervention of Madrid; at that time the Catalan Left had opposed them. Now, since the Catalan Right had been defeated on July 19th together with the fascist Generals, the Catalan Left demands the intervention of the central government in Catalan affairs. In both cases, the interests and privileges of property, of capitalism, were being defended. In both cases they fought against the workers who were striving for the Social Revolution. The orchestra leader had been changed, but the music was the same.

EVENTS IN THE PROVINCES

What happened in the provinces of Catalonia proves that the entire movement was organised to destroy the CNT and the FAI and, with them, the revolutionary achievements of the 19th of July.

The various towns and villages of Catalonia reported to the Regional Committee on what happened. These reports show the counter-revolutionary character of the movement. At Montesquieu, Lafarga, and Bisaura the members of the CNT were persecuted and even driven away. Sixty anarchist refugees from the neighbouring villages came to Vich.

In the Tortosa district, unmotivated attacks were launched against the economic institutions of the workers. The incidents were particularly indecent at La Cenia. Two hundred assault guards occupied the village on May 7th. The guards entered the Union headquarters of the CNT and destroyed everything they could lay their hands on. Eight people, men and women, who were in the union quarters at the time, were arrested. The headquarters of the Libertarian Youth was occupied, its furniture destroyed. The collective economic enterprises were dissolved, their quarters occupied by the assault guards with the assistance of the bourgeois republican elements and members of the PSUC. This action was directed against the economic achievements of the proletariat. The comrades report from La Cenia:

"Our Collective, consisting of 450 members has been a model for the entire district. For seven months we have made economic sacrifices in order to build up our Collective. We have done away with the wage system, have established a just distribution. We had a cooperative barber shop, cooperative kitchens and a big coffee house. The capital invested by the workers, and the stock on hand was worth 45,000 pesetas. All this has been taken away from us, so that our families are now starving. Our barber shop had ten modern chairs. These, as well as our stock of textiles and our collective stable of work horses have been taken away from us. They even went so far as to invade the homes of our comrades and rob them of clothing and money. Forty comrades have been arrested and were taken to Tortosa. Sixty civil guards remained in the village after they had finished their thefts. They are still occupying everything. We beg the comrades to send us help soon, because we fear they will take everything away from us, even our supply of oil, worth 140,000 pesetas."

At Amettla de Mar not only were workers molested, but also the militiamen who had membership *carnets* of the CNT. The secretary of the CNT unions was arrested, and his position as a member of the Municipal Council taken over by a member of the PSUC and UGT.

At Tortosa the repression was even worse. CNT membership *carnets* were taken away from their owners and torn up. The assault guards worked together with the members of the PSUC. Syndicalist and anarchist members of the Municipality were expelled and substituted by members of the small bourgeoisie and the PSUC. Numerous arrests were made.

At Villadalan Juan Garcia, the anarchist member of the City Council was arrested and all the anarchist members of the City Council were expelled from office. The membership *carnets* and banners of the CNT were torn up.

The collectivised enterprises of the CNT in Tortosa were also the object of attacks on the part of the united reactionary forces. The movement was directed against the social achievements of the proletariat. After the 19th of July the land was being cultivated collectively by the workers. The petty bourgeoisie wanted to do away with this collectivisation. A great number of assault guards and members of the bourgeois parties disarmed the workers and then proceeded to liquidate the collectivised institutions. Two tractors of the collective were returned to their former owners.

The inhabitants of Amposta were compelled to surrender their arms to the assault guards. This action was in no way justified. The people were going about their daily occupations. The production of rice in this village since July 19th, amounted to 40,000.000 kilos, and the community had put this at the disposal of the Republic.

There were no differences between the CNT and the UGT here. Both organisations sent a delegate to Barcelona to request the Government to remove the troops. When the delegation reached Tortosa, the CNT representative was arrested. A new delegation was sent to Tortosa to secure the release of the arrested comrade. Without success. Later Amposta was occupied by civil guards. The workers gave up their arms, and shortly afterward, the civil guards distributed these arms among the Socalist Youth (members of the PSUC youth organisation). Arrests were made; and ten days later, five of the arrested were still in prison in Tortosa.

EVENTS IN TARRAGONA

On May 5th, at eight o'clock in the morning, the telephone exchange was occupied by a heavily armed police force. The telephone calls were censored and the telephone connections between the different sections of the CNT and the FAI cut.

At midday Comrade Casanovas, representative of the telephone workers and employees, went to the military headquarters to inform the chief of the coastal service of the occupation of the telephone exchange. They agreed, after discussions with the Chief of Police, that the police should retire from the upper floors of the building where the technical apparatus is, and remain in the hall below on guard. Later, the Chief of Police communicated that the Delegate of Public Order refused to observe the agreement, presumably following orders from Barcelona.

Shortly afterwards, a number of people were seen entering the headquarters of the left republican parties unarmed, and leaving equipped with rifles. The same thing was going on at the headquarters of the Socialist Youth: Casa del Pueblo. The comrades of the anarchist and anarcho-syndicalist organisations also began to gather in their centres and prepare for their defence.

Between 6 and 7 o'clock the following morning, the headquarters of the Libertarian Youth was attacked with hand grenades and rifles. After 15 minutes the attacking forces retired, apparently obeying orders. At 11 o'clock a commission of the CNT and the FAI went to the Generality and demanded a meeting of all antifascist organisations. The Generality acceded to this demand, but the representatives of the UGT and PSUC refused to attend.

Heavy fire broke out again at half past three in front of the headquarters of the Libertarian Youth, which was now being attacked by both police and civilian forces. A new commission of the CNT-FAI demanded that the Generality call a meeting of all the antifascist organisations. The Chief of Aviation at Reus had taken over public security. The CNT and the FAI informed him that they did not want to shed any blood and therefore wanted a conference of all antifascist organisations. At last the Conference took place. The Chief of Aviation declared that he had orders to proceed against the CNT-FAI by force if they did not immediately surrender all their arms.

Our comrades decided to give up their arms in order to avoid further bloodshed and destruction of homes, under the following conditions:

1. Release of all the imprisoned.
2. Withdrawal of the armed police and all other armed formations. Members of the Air Force were to take their place.
3. The life and liberty of all comrades, as well as their homes, to be respected.

The comrades of the CNT-FAI turned over all their arms to Captain Barbete himself in the headquarters of the Transport Union. The captain noticed and remarked on the fact that the weapons had not been used at all. He congratulated the comrades of the CNT on their sensible conduct. Arms were also given up to the police at the CNT headquarters.

And still there was no calm. About three o'clock in the morning, assault guards and police attacked the headquarters of the Ministry of Defence.

The persecutions against the militants and comrades of the CNT-FAI first began then. Thus, once more, the authorities and political organisations broke their promises.

Following are the names of comrades who were found murdered in various places outside the city: Mario Berruti, Baltasar Ballejo, Mateo Freixas, José Gallisa, and Julian Martinez from Figueras. The last three had been arrested and taken to the police station. From there, assault guards took them to an unknown destination. Two hours later their corpses were identified in the morgue of the cemetery. Four other bodies could not be identified, but we must assume that they were also comrades of the CNT and the FAI.

Many houses of our comrades have been searched. These searches were carried out by the police and members of the Communist and Catalan Nationalist Parties. On May 7th, at a quarter past nine in the morning the merchant, Gisbert, appeared at the quarters of the cooperative stores of the CNT accompanied by the merchants, José Luis and Juan Galvet, and the railwaymen, Roche and Llacer, and obliged the personnel at gunpoint to stop working. The personnel and clients were compelled to leave the shop while the intruders remained behind as victors. A truckload of goods was stolen.

After the airborne troops had retired, assault guards and members of the Communist and Catalan Nationalist Parties invaded the headquarters of the CNT. They forced the doors open and destroyed the furniture. Thefts were committed in all the CNT local branches. One Recasens, member of the Esquerra, tried to assassinate a wounded comrade, Balabasque, member of the Libertarian Youth, in the City Hospital. The murder was prevented by members of the hospital. But when the brute threatened to kill Balabasque after he had recovered, the wounded man died from the shock of the entire incident within two hours.

It is obvious, from the narrative of these days, that the anarchists and syndicalists did not initiate a putsch. The workers were not interested in any internal struggle among the antifascist parties. On the contrary, it was in their interest to maintain the antifascist front.

It is also false to speak of uncontrolled elements having started the fighting, and, by that, mean the anarchists and syndicalists. The Paris evening paper, *Ce Soir*, makes this mistake out of sheer ignorance. In its edition of May 6th, it says: "The Generality is master of the situation. Some of the suburbs still seem to be in the hands of the enemy. Who are these enemies? It seems that the rebellion was started by some uncontrollable elements who managed to get into the most extreme wing of the anarchist movement in order to provoke disturbances in favour of the enemies of the republic."

The Spanish press also spoke of uncontrolled elements, and referred to the anarchists. Every conceivable crime and excess was attributed to them, thereby covering the activities of the members of the PSUC and the Estat Catalá, who were committing the most horrible atrocities. Here is an example of an incident in which truly uncontrolled elements indulged: During the tragic days, twelve militants of the anarchist youth were going from the suburb Armonia del Palomar to the offices of the Regional

Committee. Near the city park they were stopped and taken to the Karl Marx Barracks, belonging to the PSUC. They simply disappeared. This took place on May 4th. Four days later, on May 9th, a mysterious ambulance left twelve terribly mutilated bodies on the road between Bella Terra and Sardanola Ripolet. The corpses were identified as those of the twelve young anarchists from Armonia del Palomar. These are the names of some of them. Cesar, Fernandez Nari, Jose Villena, Juan Antonio y Luis Carnera.

Other examples could be cited. They prove that the rising was not started by the anarchists, and that the uncontrolled elements must be sought in other quarters. To blame the anarchists is either to distort the truth, or pure fantasy. *La Noche* of May 7th, remarks on the following incident:

"An evening paper published a false sensational story about something that occurred in the headquarters of the CNT-FAI. This paper writes: 'We learn that certain incidents occurred in the Casa CNT-FAI this morning. Some elements were expressing their dissatisfaction with the policies of the Confederation and provoked conflicts that resulted in a number of casualties. Ambulances arrived to take the wounded away.'

La Noche continues: "Since we know about said incident we wish to correct the mistake. On Wednesday morning, a well-known printer, with premises in the Calle Nueva de la Rambla, came to the Red Cross station on Calle Casanova. He asked for an ambulance to go to the rescue of his child who had been bitten by a mad dog. Owing to the tragic situation, the Red Cross could not spare an ambulance. However the delegate of the transport workers union of the CNT offered to help the man. An ambulance took them to the headquarters of the CNT nearby, where some rather heavy shooting was going on. The Regional Committee of the CNT put a car at the disposal of the despairing father, who was thus able to get help for his child...There was no conflict and no wounded at the Casa CNT-FAI. Only an act of humanity on the part of the comrades of the CNT."

Peace was restored among the warring brothers. The CNT, as usual, kept to the agreement which it had accepted. Their militants put down their arms. They went back to work and did everything to prove their willingness to re-establish peace. They left their strategic positions. They started to tear down their barricades. Nothing must remain as a reminder of this tragic fratricidal struggle.

The same cannot be said of the workers' opponents. The members of the Catalan Nationalists, as well as some uncontrolled elements of the PSUC and of the UGT considered themselves the victors. Protected by the old Catalan guards, who had not been disbanded, and by the new troops from Valencia, they dared to go into the streets, and stop workers, individually or in small groups, and, if they belonged to the CNT or the FAI, insult them, tear off their insignias and rip up their membership books. The new chief of police gave orders that people were not to be stopped in the street any more. They ignored it. Uniformed and non uniformed, partly illegal, guards continued to stop the workers. Every day new incidents were occurring. Here is one example:

On Sunday night, May 9th, after two days of calm, some uncontrolled elements of the UGT took advantage of the deserted condition of the city at 10 p.m. to send a number of men from their metal workers union, located on the Calle Diputacion to the headquarters of the theatrical workers union of the CNT, opposite them. They had chosen an hour when they expected no resistance. Our comrades were there, but decided not to resist. They called up the Executive Committee of the UGT and asked them to call back their uncontrolled and undisciplined members from the offices of a CNT union. On Thursday, May 15th, the headquarters were still occupied.

An even more vivid example: The Union of Liberal Professions of the CNT, art section, had opened an art exhibition in their headquarters. These were paintings saved by the anarchists during the early days of destruction. In the course of the fighting, some uncontrolled members of the PSUC broke into the exhibition hall with guns and revolvers drawn. The artists who were present did not want to start a bloody battle. The uncontrolled elements took possession of their quarters as well as of the exhibition. The pistoleros of the rebels reigned over the cultural centres of the anarchists. The anarchists, were they the men of blood and cruelty they are reported to be in Spain as well as abroad, would have proceeded to recapture the building. They rejected such a step. They did not want to risk the destruction of the art treasures they had rescued on the 19th of July. Their responsible Committees preferred to intervene with the official government to have their exhibition cleared of the intruders.

According to the pact, the prisoners were supposed to be released immediately by both sides. The comrades of the CNT and the FAI remained true to their word. They were self-disciplined and immediately released hundreds of prisoners, most of whom had put themselves under the protection of the anarchists voluntarily. Their opponents were not so faithful to their promises. Long negotiations were required before the communists and the Catalan nationalists would release their anarchist prisoners. A full week after the re-establishment of normality, many members of the CNT and the FAI were still being held. On the 13th of May, the anarchists, Cosme Paules del Roro, José Domínguez, Antonio Ignacil, Francisco Sarqueda are still imprisoned in the Karl Marx Barracks, while Miguel Castells, José Degá, Alvaro Galcerán, José Luis García, Manuel Horno, José Lucio Gómez, Eulogio Marqués Romero and Antonio Sánchez are still being held in the offices of the Central Committee of the PSUC (Pedrera). In the headquarters of the Estat Catalá, in the Rambla Catalonia, Miguel Piqué Ibáñez, José Rovira and Ramón Robello, all militants of the CNT and the FAI are still detained. 200 militants of the CNT-FAI are still prisoners in the police jail. Many have been arrested in the Palace of the Generality and are still being held: and others have disappeared, no one knowing whether they are being held by the PSUC or the Estat Catalá.

3

Barcelona: The May Events
Burnett Bolloten

The dynamics of the political conflict in Barcelona were now leading inexorably toward open warfare, toward that bloody episode and turning point in the Spanish Revolution known as the May days or May events.

Seizing the initiative, Rodríguez Salas, the PSUC police commissioner, made a daring move. At 3 P.M. on Monday, 3 May, accompanied by three truckloads of assault guards, and acting in concert with Aiguadé, the Esquerra councillor of internal security, he raided the central telephone exchange, which the CNT had occupied since the defeat of the military in July and regarded as a "key position in the Revolution."[1] Swiftly entering the ten-story building, the assault guards occupied the ground floor, but were stopped when they reached one of the upper floors.[2]

In accordance with the Catalan government's decree on collectivization and workers' control of 24 October 1936 that legalized the sequestration or control of the larger commercial and industrial concerns seized by the unions during the first days of the Revolution, the telephone exchange, owned by the Compañía Telefónica Nacional de España, a subsidiary of the International Telephone and Telegraph Corporation, was controlled by a committee of the CNT and UGT. On this body the anarchosyndicalists were the dominant force, and their red and black flag, which had flown from the tower of the building ever since July, attested to their supremacy.

Although, in accordance with the decree, the committee was presided over by a government delegate, his presence merely created an illusion of official control where in reality none existed. "Serious things were going on there that the government had to end," declared

Juan Comorera, the PSUC secretary. "All the interior controls of the telephone exchange were in the service, not of the community, but of one organization, and neither President Azaña nor President Companys, nor anyone else, could speak without an indiscreet controller overhearing."[3] This was no exaggeration. It was precisely for the purpose of intercepting conversations that the CNT had placed "interventors" or controllers in the building. President Companys himself, in his notes on the May events, testifies that "all the telephone calls of the Generalitat authorities, of the President of Catalonia and of the President of the Republic were intercepted."[4] If this interception was not a prerogative bestowed by law, it was nonetheless, in the opinion of the CNT, an indefeasible right conferred by the Revolution. In its ability to interpose its veto, to intercept, as the FAI leader, Abad de Santillán, puts it, "compromising messages and conversations" and to overhear persons "conspiring to whittle away the people's rights,"[5] the CNT possessed a vital element of real power, that neither the PSUC nor the Esquerra could permit for long if they were ever to be masters of the region.

Thus, when Rodríguez Salas raided the central telephone exchange with an order signed by Aiguadé,[6] it is not unlikely that he had the tacit if not formal approval of most of the members of the government except those belonging to the CNT.[7] One other notable exception, however, was the shrewd and extremely circumspect premier of the Catalan government, José Tarradellas. According to President Azaña —who, it will be recalled, had fled to Barcelona in October 1936 in order to be near the French border[8]—Tarradellas told him on the first night of the fighting that he had learned of the raid only after the order had been given and that he considered the decision "hazardous," because the government lacked resources with which to subdue any resistance it might encounter.[9] "He criticized Aiguadé a lot," Azaña further testifies, "for having launched a battle without preparing for it, and Companys for talking so much about doing battle, as a result of which he had alarmed the anarchists. He believed that ultimately everything would be settled through negotiation."[10]

On learning of the raid, the CNT councillors demanded the removal of both Rodríguez Salas and Aiguadé, but to no avail.[11] "The intransigence of the other parties," writes José Peirats, the anarchosyndicalist historian, "and especially the opportunist attitude of the president of the Generalitat, who resolutely opposed this punishment, provoked a general strike followed by an outbreak of hostilities."[12]

In a retrospective account of the May events, Manuel Cruells, a staff reporter at the time on the *Diari de Barcelona*, the organ of Estat Catalá, representing the small separatist movement among the Catalan middle classes, states: "If Companys had adopted an energetic attitude by removing his councillor of the interior and the general commissar of public order, as logically he should have done, there would have been no tragic week of May in Barcelona. . . . It is somewhat difficult to understand the attitude of President Companys under the particular circumstances. . . . Either he was badly informed and did not realize how grave the situation might become as a result of his refusal, or he was well informed and acquiesced in provoking the serious situation. . . . Why did the president not insist on the proposed resignations? Had he allowed himself to be carried away by the anti-FAI hysteria that had already begun to manifest itself in the streets? Did he wish to be loyal, as on other occasions, to certain friends in his own party? It is difficult to explain the real cause of the president's attitude, but we can affirm that it was decisive in sparking the conflict, suffused with hate, that Barcelona had to endure."[13]

As news of the raid on the telephone building became known, anger swept through the working-class districts, mainly anarchosyndicalist. "Hundreds of comrades occupy the streets," wrote an anarchist eyewitness. "They wish to go to the center of the city and make a CLEAN SWEEP of those who want to repeat the fascist provocation of 19 July. They are restrained with difficulty. The comrades . . . know what the aggressors are seeking. . . . What they want is to strangle the Revolution, destroy the conquests of the revolutionary workers, and simply reestablish the bourgeois democratic Republic. To achieve this goal it is necessary to provoke the anarchists into a conflict, declare them enemies of the 'Popular Front' government, destroy their organizations, open the way to intervention by the democratic capitalist powers, and drown the onward march of the revolutionary Spanish workers in blood. The so-called 'workers' fatherland' is an accomplice in this executioners' job against the Revolution and is sacrificing the future liberty of the Spanish people for the help the democratic capitalist powers offer against the fascist threat to its existence."[14]

Hundreds of barricades were rapidly erected. "The building of these barricades was a strange and wonderful sight," wrote George Orwell, an eyewitness in the Ramblas, one of the main avenues. "With the kind of passionate energy that Spaniards display when they have definitely decided to begin upon any object of work, long lines of men, women, and quite small children were tearing up cobblestones, hauling them along in a handcart that had been found somewhere, and staggering to and fro under heavy sacks of sand."[15]

Before nightfall Barcelona was an armed camp. "Thousands upon thousands of workers have returned to the streets with arms in their hands," declared the POUM executive. "Plants, machine shops, warehouses have stopped work. The barricades of liberty have risen again in every part of town. The spirit of July has once more taken possession of Barcelona."[16]

In a great ring around Barcelona extending from the working-class suburbs to the edge of the commercial and official section of the city, the anarchosyndicalists were masters of the situation. Inside the business and political enclave, however, the opposing forces were fairly evenly matched. For example, in the Plaza de Cataluña, the central square, where the anarchosyndicalists held the *telefónica*, the PSUC was entrenched in the Hotel Colón, its headquarters, which it had sequestered in July, and from whose windows almost the entire square could be swept by machine-gun fire.

In the working-class suburbs of Sarriá, Hostafrancs, and Sans, as well as the maritime quarter of Barceloneta, the assault and national republican guards were powerless.[17] Some surrendered without resistance, while others remained in their barracks, waiting to see how the crisis would run its course. "Instantaneously, nearly the whole of Barcelona was in the power of our armed groups," affirms the FAI leader Abad de Santillán. "They did not move from their posts, although they could have done so easily and overcome the small centers of resistance."[18] Had the CNT and FAI been interested in taking power, he asserted, their victory would have been complete, "but this did not interest us, for it would have been an act of folly contrary to our principles of unity and democracy."[19]

Near the Catalan Parliament building, where President Azaña had recently established his official residence, intermittent firing was going on. At 8 P.M., he instructed his secretary general, Cándido Bolívar, then in Valencia, to request Premier Largo Caballero for reinforcements to bolster his presidential guard. Caballero had retired even earlier than usual, and Bolívar brought the ruffled premier out of bed at 8:30 P.M. After urging him to dispatch additional forces without delay, Bolívar departed, little suspecting that his request would remain unheeded.[20] Shortly afterward interior minister Galarza informed Caballero that Aiguadé had asked for the "urgent dispatch of 1,500 guards, indispensable for suppressing the movement."[21]

At 11 P.M. Premier Tarradellas, acting on behalf of President Companys, visited Azaña to offer his apologies for the state of turbulence. The normally short trip of only a few minutes from the Generalitat Palace to the Parliament building had taken an hour and a half. "He had been obliged to descend from his car at every barricade . . . to parley at length, and had been humiliated," Azaña notes in his memoirs. "When he began to make excuses [for the turmoil], stressing the fact that, as a Catalan, he felt ashamed, I interrupted him and repeated the remarks I had made to Bolívar to pass on to the prime minister. 'Don't make excuses! Suppress the insurrection! As far as I am concerned, guarantee my safety and my freedom of movement.'" Tarradellas then took leave of the president, who heard nothing more from the Catalan government during the rest of the fighting. "No one in the Generalitat asked about me, or tried to speak to me, or concerned himself with my position," he remarks bitterly. "It was more than a scandalous discourtesy; it was an act of silent hostility." Nor did Prime Minister Largo Caballero concern himself with the president's plight. "He neither called me nor sent me any message."[22]

"The whole night [3–4 May] the rebels were masters of the city," Azaña continues. "They raised barricades, occupied buildings and important points without anyone interfering with them. . . . I was not worried, but I was disturbed by the position they had put me in. I perceived vaguely that the conflict did not directly involve me, and I even thought that if things got worse it might help to achieve peace [in Spain]. What disgusted me and annoyed me was the scandal the rebellion would create abroad, the benefit the other rebels would derive from it, and its repercussions upon the war."[23]

That same night the executive committee of the POUM met with the regional committees of the CNT, FAI, and Libertarian Youth. Julián Gorkin, a member of the executive, recalls: "We stated the problem in these precise terms: 'Neither of us has urged the masses of Barcelona to take this action. This is a spontaneous response to a Stalinist provocation. This is the decisive moment for the Revolution. Either we place ourselves at the head of the movement in order to destroy the internal enemy or else the movement will collapse and the enemy will destroy us. We must make our choice; revolution or counterrevolution.' [The regional committees] made no decision. Their maximum demand was the removal of the [police] commissioner who had provoked the movement. As though it were not the various forces behind him that had to be destroyed! Always the form instead of the substance! . . . Our party placed itself on the side of the movement, even though we knew it was condemned to failure."[24]

The following morning, Tuesday, 4 May, Aiguadé repeated his request for fifteen hundred assault guards, but interior minister Galarza, acting on instructions from Largo Caballero, gave only a temporizing reply. "I have ordered the concentration of [police] forces in Castellón, Murcia, Alicante, and Valencia," he responded, "and, in case of necessity, should serious clashes occur in Catalonia . . . the necessary forces will be placed at your disposal. But the *premier and I agree that while everything should be prepared* the intervention of forces not stationed in Catalonia is undesirable, so long as those already there do not have to be employed to the full and have not been proved inadequate."[25] By temporizing, Largo Caballero hoped that the fighting would subside without government intervention. Waging a political battle for survival against the Communists, he was not inclined to antagonize the CNT and FAI or to strengthen the hand of his opponents in Catalonia by sending reinforcements to the region.

Meanwhile, the situation in Barcelona was deteriorating. The rattle of machine-gun fire, the explosion of hand grenades and dynamite, and the fire of mortars merged into a single roar. This "devilish noise," wrote Orwell, "echoing from thousands of stone buildings, went on and on and on, like a tropical rainstorm. Crack-crack, rattle-rattle, roar—sometimes it died away to a few shots, sometimes it quickened to a deafening fusillade, but it never stopped while daylight lasted."[26] Although isolated attempts were made to capture enemy strongholds, there was comparatively little fighting in the open. Most of the combatants remained in buildings or behind barricades and blazed away at their enemies opposite.[27]

"We realized that what was happening was that everybody's house was burning," declared Abad de Santillán some days later, "and that the only hope under the circumstances was to extinguish the flames and end the bloody slaughter."[28] A few months later, however, he had second thoughts: "Perhaps . . . we allowed ourselves to be guided much more by a sense of loyalty and generosity than by a precise understanding of the plot that had been hatched against us."[29]

At 2 P.M. the CNT and FAI appealed over the radio for a cease-fire: "Workers! . . . We are not responsible for what is happening. We are attacking no one. We are only defending oursleves. . . . Lay down your arms! Remember, we are brothers! . . . If we fight among ourselves we are doomed to defeat."[30]

But there were forces intent on stoking the conflict. Not only were Rodríguez Salas's men initiating new offensive actions, but the tiny Trotskyist group of Bolshevik Leninists and the dissident anarchists of the Friends of Durruti, joined by a few of the more militant members of the POUM, were extremely active.

The attitude of the POUM leaders, on the other hand, was pessimistic. As Julián Gorkin recalled, "We placed ourselves on the side of the movement, even though we knew it was condemned to failure."[31] "We did not feel ourselves spiritually or physically strong enough to take the lead in organizing the masses for resistance," a member of the executive acknowledged.[32] And George Orwell, a participant in the fighting and a POUM sympathizer, corroborates: "Those who were in personal touch with the POUM leaders at the time have told me that they were in reality dismayed by the whole business, but felt that they had got to associate themselves with it."[33]

The leadership did not publicly display its pessimism and on the surface appeared combative despite its unsuccessful overtures to the regional committees of the libertarian movement on the night of 3 May for joint, aggressive action. The next morning, *La Batalla* urged the workers to remain in "a state of permanent mobilization" and to "prosecute and intensify the offensive that has been initiated as there is no better means of defense than attack. It is imperative to demand and obtain the resignation of the general commissioner of public order. . . . It is imperative to demand and obtain the abrogation of the decrees on public order adopted by reaction and reformism. To achieve all this and to continue the revolutionary action, broadening its scope every day and carrying it to its ultimate consequences, it is imperative that the working class, remaining in a state of mobilization and on the offensive, should form the Revolutionary Workers' Front and should proceed immediately with the organization of committees in defense of the Revolution."[34]

In Valencia, that same morning, Tuesday, 4 May, Premier Largo Caballero, fearing that the Communists might exploit the fighting to topple his government, summoned the CNT ministers. Aiguadé, the Catalan councillor of internal security, he told them, had asked the minister of the interior to dispatch fifteen hundred assault guards. "The government," he argued, "could not do that because it would mean placing forces in the service of the person who may possibly have had something to do with the conflict. Before acceding, he would take over the administration of public order as provided in the Constitution."[35] He therefore suggested that representatives of the national committee of the CNT and of the executive committee of the UGT should leave for Barcelona immediately to try to end the hostilities.[36] A meeting of the national committee was then summoned, at which it was decided to send representatives to Barcelona "so as to avoid the taking over of public order by the central government."[37] Mariano Vázquez, CNT secretary, and García Oliver, CNT minister of justice, were designated by the committee, while Carlos Hernández Zancajo and Mariano Muñoz Sánchez, both supporters of Largo Caballero, were appointed by the UGT executive.[38]

At 11 A.M. the central government met. Backed by Indalecio Prieto and by the Left Republican ministers, the Communists pressed the premier to take immediate action, demanding not only that reinforcements be dispatched to Catalonia, but that the government assume control of public order and of military affairs in the region. Succumbing to the threat of a cabinet crisis, Caballero reluctantly agreed to adopt these measures, but only if the situation did not improve by evening.

At 1:10 P.M. President Companys—who had undoubtedly instructed Aiguadé to request the fifteen hundred assault guards from Valencia —informed Largo Caballero that the situation was "very serious," that the police forces were "inadequate for rapid action and are becoming exhausted."[39] Caballero replied: "I deem it my duty to inform you that . . . all [the ministers] have decided that if the situation does not improve *by an early hour this evening*, the government will assume control of public order in accordance with the Statute [of Catalan Autonomy]. Tell me if you have any objection."[40] This was an extremely delicate question for President Companys—the chief custodian of regional autonomy—who certainly would have preferred the dispatch of reinforcements to the sacrifice of Catalan autonomy. But, fearful lest he be denied the much-needed forces unless he surrendered the control of public order, he responded: *"I believe that [the central government] should cooperate in strengthening the available forces* of the councillor of internal security." But, then, with resignation, he added, "In view of the danger that the [state of public order] may get worse the government of the Republic can adopt the measures it deems necessary."[41]

In a written statement, signed on 9 August 1946 in the presence of several Catalan refugees, Jaime Antón Aiguadé, the nephew of Artemio Aiguadé, alleges that his uncle told him that President Companys surrendered the control of public order to Valencia without either consulting him or the Catalan government. He further alleges that, according to his uncle, Companys's pleas for reinforcements were inspired by Juan Comorera, the PSUC leader, who, "during those days did not move for a single moment from Companys's side, giving him advice and taking advantage of the moral depression of the president to propose solutions that suited the interests of the PSUC." It was Comorera, the document claims, who suggested to Companys that he "accept the solution proposed by the government of Valencia."[42]

However this may be, there can be little doubt that President Companys had the tacit support of other leaders of the Esquerra, including that of Aiguadé himself, when he agreed to surrender the control of public order to Valencia, and that the document in question was a palpable attempt—during a period of postwar dissensions within the Esquerra—to lay the historic responsibility for the loss of Catalan autonomy solely at the door of Companys and the PSUC.

Despite Companys's go-ahead, Premier Largo Caballero was not yet willing to act. He was still hoping that his emissaries in Barcelona might end the bloodshed by mediation. But Indalecio Prieto, his Socialist rival and navy and air minister, did wish to take action. An irreconcilable opponent of the CNT and FAI, he believed from the inception of the Revolution, according to his own account, that the most important task of the republican government was to recover the reins of power.[43] He instructed air force chief Ignacio Hidalgo de Cisneros to proceed to the Catalan air base at Reus with a detachment of ground forces for its defense and with two bomber and two fighter squadrons "for operations against the region in the event the insurrectionists should win."[44] Furthermore, in reply to a succession of teletyped messages from Manuel Azaña requesting with "hysterical insistence"—as one witness put it—that steps be taken for his personal protection,[45] Prieto ordered two destroyers, the *Lepanto* and *Sánchez Barcaiztegui*, to sail for Barcelona with marines to evacuate the president. "I have already stated," Azaña records in his memoirs, "that the prime minister did not attempt to communicate with me either directly or indirectly. Nor did he inform the ministers of my situation. Prieto got in touch with me by telegraph on Tuesday, midmorning. He was aware of the tumult in Barcelona, but . . . he could not fully appreciate my position without seeing it. He told me that he was sending two destroyers to the port of Barcelona . . . to be placed at my disposal; that twenty airplanes would leave for Reus and Prat; that the ministries of the interior and war were sending two armed units, and that one thousand air force soldiers were being flown to Reus. He was very alarmed and ready to crush the rebellion."[46]

All day Tuesday the government in Valencia remained in continuous session. In the late afternoon Largo Caballero's opponents reminded him of the commitment he had made earlier in the day to assume control of public order and military affairs in Catalonia if the situation did not improve by the evening. During the entire day, the CNT and FAI in Barcelona had kept up their appeals for a cease-fire. At 3 P.M. they had exhorted over the radio: "Workers of the CNT, workers of the UGT! Do not put up with deceit and trickery. Above all let us unite. Lay down your arms! Heed only one slogan: Everyone back to work to defeat fascism!"[47] Despite these appeals, wrote Agustín Souchy, the AIT representative in Casa CNT-FAI, anarchosyndicalist head-quarters, the hostilities could not be contained. "Rancor increased on all sides."[48]

While the cabinet debate in Valencia was still in progress, *Frente Rojo*, the Communist evening newspaper, declared: "For a long time we used to attribute anything that occurred to gangs euphemistically called 'uncontrollables.' Now we see that they are perfectly controlled . . . but by the enemy. This cannot be tolerated any longer. . . . There has been enough indulgence already. There is a limit to patience. When the existence of Spain as an independent nation is at stake, when the liberty of the Spanish people and the well-being and future of the popular masses is in jeopardy, we cannot allow ourselves to be stabbed in the back. . . . There can be no more discussion on these matters. We must act. And with the severity that circumstances de-mand. . . . All those who attempt, in one form or another, with some aim or another, to disturb [order] or break [discipline] should imme-diately feel the ruthless weight of popular authority, repression by the government, and punitive action by the popular masses."[49]

Inside the cabinet the debate assumed a rabid character. "Comrade Federica Montseny," said the CNT, "led the opposition for four hours against the Communists and republicans who supported the taking over of public order and defense. It was a tumultuous debate, which we lost when the vote was taken."[59] It was decided, however, that the measures would not be put into effect until the last moment,[51] a condition wrung by Montseny and Caballero from their opponents in the belief that the CNT and UGT representatives now en route to Bar-celona might negotiate a peaceful settlement.

On their arrival, the emissaries from Valencia joined the Catalan leaders in the Generalitat Palace in appealing for a cease-fire. Mariano Vázquez, the CNT secretary, urged his embattled followers to remem-ber the neighboring Aragon front, where "the fascists might attack at any moment."[52] García Oliver, the CNT-FAI leader and minister of justice, declared: "Think of the pain, think of the anguish . . . of those antifascist workers in that part of Spain dominated by the whip of Hitler and Mussolini when they learn . . . that in [Catalonia] we are killing one another. . . . All of you should remain in your respective positions . . . but should cease firing, even though provoked by persons not interested in finding a solution to this conflict. . . . [I] declare that the guards who have died today are my brothers. I kneel before them and kiss them. . . . [All] those who have died today are my brothers. I kneel before them and kiss them."[53]

That some libertarians were incensed by their leaders' appeals for a cease-fire is confirmed by anarchist sources. "It should not surprise anyone," observed an eyewitness, "that when our representatives, who went to the Generalitat [Palace] to arrange a settlement, gave the order 'Cease Fire!' there were some comrades who felt, in their indignation, that it was a form of treachery to allow those assassins [a reference to the PSUC members and assault guards firing near Casa CNT-FAI] to escape without just punishment."[54]

There was also dissension among the leaders. Helmut Ruediger, vice-secretary of the AIT, who was active in Barcelona at the time of the May events, testifies:

The problem as to whether the CNT should "go the whole way," taking into its own hands the reins of power, or should continue to collaborate was raised several times after the militants had decided in favor of collaboration on 19 July. The decision of 19 July was unanimous, although spontaneous. Not everyone realized what it signified. But it was during the May days, in particular, during the stormy meetings in Casa CNT-FAI in Barcelona, while the deafening noise of rifle and machine-gun fire could be heard on every side, that more than once the question—which finally received a negative response—was raised: "Should we or should we not *take power*?" It was in these terms that the representatives of the organization summed up the problem during those bloody days. But being *anarchists*, what did they mean by "power"?

Let us first agree as to what they definitely *did not* mean. Anarchism and revolutionary syndicalism have never seen in state power, in government, with its administrative and repressive machinery, the means of realizing the social changes they desire. Nor were they of the opinion that the basic condition of Socialist construction should be the erection of a new fascist-Stalinist style totalitarian superstate. They maintained that the social revolution should dispense with *both* the bourgeois state and the new totalitarian superstate, and that social reorganization, like the defense of the Revolution, should be concentrated in the hands of *working-class organizations*—whether labor unions or new organs of spontaneous creation, such as free councils, etc., which, as an expression of the will of the workers themselves, from *below up*, should construct the new social community, thus discarding all conventional forms of authoritarian "power" exercised from above.

But in view of the fact that on 3 May the CNT, representing the majority of the Catalan industrial workers, was in open conflict with *all* organizations comprising the other social layers . . . (the small bourgeoisie, the intellectuals, the *immense mass* of the Catalan peasants, namely, the *rabassaires* [sharecroppers], white-collar workers, technicians, etc.) the question of "power" meant *whether the CNT at that time should crush them all, concentrate the leadership of public affairs in its own hands, and create its own repressive apparatus necessary to prevent the "crushed" from returning to public life.* The reply was "no," but the decisions of those tragic days later provoked a whirlwind of discussions, mutual recriminations, and struggles within the Spanish and international libertarian movement.[55]

At about 9:30 Tuesday night, shortly after the appeals for a cease-fire had been broadcast from the Generalitat Palace, the emissaries from Valencia met with members of the Catalan government under the chairmanship of Companys. "We proposed the formula that a provisional council [government] should be set up, composed of four representatives, [Esquerra, CNT, UGT, and Unió de Rabassaires] in which no one who had belonged to any of the previous governments should participate," said the CNT. "In this way, we would remove Aiguadé and Rodríguez Salas, because we stipulated that the new councillor of internal security should assume absolute [that is, personal] control of public order." This proposal was accepted. But when the CNT suggested that the new government should be formed immediately "so that . . . public opinion would know that the conflict had been resolved," the Communists maintained that "it was first of all essential that the firing in the streets should cease." The CNT representatives tried to hold their ground. "We believed it was necessary to gain time to prevent the [central] government from having to assume control of public order, but no agreement was possible. Although the Esquerra and the Unió de Rabassaires did not join in the debate, they supported the Communist point of view. Finally, at 2 A.M. [Wednesday, 5 May], the meeting ended with a decision to announce over the radio . . . that we had reached agreement and that firing should cease completely in order to normalize the situation. . . . When the meeting was over we informed the [central] government that things were going well."[56]

Encouraged by this news, Largo Caballero announced before dawn that the government had approved "the necessary decrees for rapidly resolving the situation in Catalonia, but believes that their implementation will not now be necessary and that order will be restored in Barcelona today."[57] Vain hope! "During the remainder of the night," observed President Companys in his personal notes, "hard fighting continued in the streets, and the rapid dispatch of reinforcements was demanded by [the council of] internal security, by the Presidencia [the office of President Companys] and also by Vidiella [the PSUC leader]."[58]

The CNT leaders redoubled their efforts early Wednesday morning to quiet their following. "We threw into the balance all our influence, constantly sending delegations to the places where incidents were occurring."[59] But their efforts were not always well received. "I heard some comrades cry with rage over the telephone," recalls Abad de Santillán, "when they telephoned the [CNT-FAI] committees and the latter told them not to shoot, even though they were being attacked by machine-gun fire."[60]

Meanwhile, the Bolshevik Leninists and the Friends of Durruti did what they could to keep tempers afire and to give some direction to the fighting.[61] "No compromise!" declared a leaflet distributed on the barricades by the Bolshevik Leninists. "This is the decisive moment. Next time it will be too late. . . . Long live the unity of action of the CNT-FAI-POUM."[62] "A revolutionary junta!" demanded a leaflet signed by the Friends of Durruti. "Shooting of those responsible. . . . No surrender of the streets. The Revolution before everything. We greet our comrades of the POUM who have fraternized with us on the streets. *LONG LIVE THE SOCIAL REVOLUTION! DOWN WITH THE COUNTERREVOLUTION!*"[63]

The next day, *La Batalla* printed the leaflet of the Friends of Durruti on its front page with the comment that it was of "really extraordinary interest" and that "we are very pleased to reproduce it."[64] But beyond this guarded comment, the POUM leadership kept a respectable distance between itself and the Friends of Durruti. Only the most radical elements of the party collaborated with it, but without the authority of the POUM executive. Although the executive did not join other organizations in appealing over the radio for a cease-fire,[65] it did not dissociate itself publicly from the efforts at pacification of the CNT-FAI leadership. True, *La Batalla* had urged the workers in its issue of 4 May to remain in "a state of permanent mobilization" and to "prosecute and intensify the offensive that has been initiated,"[66] but these exhortations were not repeated in subsequent issues, for the POUM felt helpless in face of the passionate and repeated appeals for a cease-fire by the anarchosyndicalist leadership.

"For four days," stated the *Spanish Revolution*, the English-language bulletin of the POUM, "the workers stood ready, vigilant and awaiting the CNT's order to attack. The order never came. . . . The National Confederation of Labor [CNT], held by the workers as the mass organization of the Revolution, recoiled before the question of workers'

power. Caught up in the reins of the government, it tried to straddle
the fence with a 'union' of the opposing forces. That is why the revolutionary workers' fight of May 3 to 7 was essentially *defensive* instead
of *offensive*. The attitude of the CNT did not fail to bring forth resistance and protests. The Friends of Durruti group brought the unanimous desire of the CNT masses to the surface, but it was not able to
take the lead."[67]

According to Felix Morrow, the American Trotskyist, one of the
most vitriolic critics of the leadership of the POUM and the CNT, this
radical language was for "export purposes" only. "In general," he
added, "*Spanish Revolution* has given English readers who could not
follow the POUM's Spanish press, a distorted picture of the POUM's
conduct; it has been a 'left face.'" "Instead [of putting itself at the
head], the POUM leadership . . . put its fate in the hands of the CNT
leadership. *Not* public proposals to the CNT for joint action made
before the masses, but a behind-the-scenes conference with the regional committee.[68] Whatever the POUM proposals were, they were
rejected. You don't agree? Then we shall say nothing about them.
And the next morning . . . *La Batalla* had not a word to say about the
POUM's proposals to the CNT, about the cowardly behavior of the
CNT leaders, their refusal to organize the defense, etc."[69]

In the interest of objectivity, it is important at this stage to quote
from "Senex," one of the principal foreign defenders of anarchosyndicalist policy during the May events. In response to Felix Morrow's
criticism of the CNT leadership in his book, *Revolution and Counter-
Revolution in Spain*, he wrote:

> It is often alleged by the revolutionary romantics of the Fourth International
> that had the Spanish workers struck out boldly for an uncompromising revo-
> lutionary line, they could have dispensed with Russian aid; the response of
> the international proletariat would have been so spontaneous, direct and
> overpowering in its effect that no government would dare to halt the flow of
> armaments to revolutionary Spain.
> This point is brought out by Felix Morrow in his analysis of the May events
> in Barcelona in 1937. . . . The CNT, according to our author, should have
> taken up the challenge of the Stalinist and bourgeois forces and made the
> ensuing struggle the starting point not only of a thoroughgoing social revolu-
> tion in Spain itself, but of a revolutionary world conflagration triumphantly
> sweeping the major countries of Europe. In other words, the CNT workers,
> upon whom rested the tremendous historic responsibility of holding the first
> line of defense against the fascists, should have thrown caution to the winds,
> indulged in a grandiloquent historic gesture, plunged recklessly into the
> adventure of breaking up the antifascist front, thus opening wide the gate to
> the fascist avalanche—and all in hope of immediately bringng about the
> world revolution. . . .

For—much to the astonishment of all of us—we are assured that the European revolution was so palpably near during the May events that it was only the reformist degeneracy of the Spanish anarchists that stopped it from proceeding along the "inevitable" stages of development envisioned by Felix Morrow and other revolutionary strategists.

It is interesting in this connection to trace the logical steps in the glib reasoning employed by the latter in order to conjure up the vision of a triumphant European revolution just waiting around the corner, ready to burst forth at the historic opportunity afforded by the May events, but hopelessly bungled up by the Catalonian anarchists.

Had the anarchist and POUM workers of Barcelona kept up their resistance against Stalinist aggression during the May days—Mr. Morrow assures us—the entire loyalist Spain would have been swept by a triumphant social revolution.

"Any attempt by the bourgeois-Stalinist bloc to gather a proletarian force would have simply precipitated the extension of the workers' state to all Loyalist Spain." But—the reader will ask—what of the well-armed communist police and military units, the flying corps mainly controlled by the Stalinists, the assault guards, the carabineros, the civil guards, many of the socialist controlled military units, the bourgeois sectors, the navy controlled by the right socialist Prieto? Would they give up without any fight? Would all those units, many of whom were drilled and trained for the specific purpose of exercising a check upon the revolutionary workers, disintegrate at the first clash with the latter? And how about the International Brigades, the preponderant majority of whom were firmly controlled by the Stalinists?

That the workers supported by the CNT units stood a good chance of victory in the case of this new civil war, can be readily granted. But this would be a Pyrrhic victory at best, for it is clear that a civil war behind the front lines resulting in the demoralization of the front and the withdrawal of the troops for the participation in this new civil war would open wide the gates to the triumphant sweep of the fascists. . . .

No one with the least knowledge of the situation will say that . . . the French and British masses of people were ready to go to war for the sake of Spain. Nor will he readily concur with Felix Morrow that had the revolutionary forces of Catalonia ousted the bourgeois parties and socialist and Stalinist elements, "the French bourgeoisie would open its borders to Spain, not for intervention but for trade enabling the new regime to secure supplies—or face immediately a revolution at home." In order to do full justice to the profundity of such a statement, one has only to bear in mind that almost half of the French proletarian organizations are under the thumb of the Stalinists and the rest are swayed by the socialists. . . . How could a civil war waged against the socialists and the Stalinists of Spain, in the face of the terrific danger of a fascist break-through at that, fire the socialist- and communist-minded workers of France to the extent of having them lay down an ultimatum to [their] own bourgeoisie demanding arms for the anarchist workers of Catalonia? And, of course, the ultimatum would have to be laid down in the face of the frenzied opposition of the trade-union leadership (socialist and communist), of both parties who would use all powerful means at their disposal to slander, villify, distort the nature of the struggle waged by the revolutionary forces of Spain.[70]

But no amount of debate on the May events will ever settle the disputes between the opposing factions. One week after the fighting had ended, a resolution of the secretariat of the Fourth International declared: "Owing to lack of serious revolutionary leadership the workers have been betrayed."[71] In June, the executive committee of the Spanish Bolshevik-Leninists stated: "The POUM leadership was not even capable of an independent policy: it clung timidly to that of the CNT and slavishly repeated its defeatist slogans."[72] And, after the war, a foreign Trotskyist wrote: "Betrayed by their organizations, abandoned and handed over to the Stalinist scoundrels, the Barcelona workers made a last heroic attempt in May 1937 to defend the conquests of 19 July. . . . Once again, a revolutionary party had a magnificent opportunity to join the rising revolutionary movement, to drive it forward and lead it to victory. But while the leading anarchists placed themselves right from the start on the other side of the barricades, the POUM joined the movement only to hold it back. In this manner, victory was presented to the Stalinist hangmen."[73]

The Communists and their supporters, on the other hand, both in Spain and abroad, in a synchronized campaign, represented the POUM's conduct differently. No sooner had the fighting ended than José Díaz, the Communist party secretary, declared that the "Trotskyists" of the POUM had inspired the "criminal putsch in Catalonia."[74] *Pravda*'s correspondent in Valencia sounded the same note, alleging that the anarchist workers had been "deceived by the Trotskyist-fascist *agents provocateurs*,"[75] while the pro-Communist John Langdon-Davies, writing in the liberal *News Chronicle* of London, stated: "This has not been an anarchist uprising. It is a frustrated putsch by the 'Trotskyist' POUM working through their controlled organizations, 'Friends of Durruti,' and the Libertarian Youth."[76] For months the campaign continued unabated. In November 1937, Georges Soria, of the French Communist *Humanité*, wrote: "The POUM was anxious to maintain the state of disorder as long as possible, for this was the order [it] had received from General Franco." The POUM, he alleged, wanted to weaken the resistance of the people so that Catalonia could not go to the aid of the Basques, then under attack by Franco's German and Italian allies. "It was further hoped that it would be possible to organize widespread propaganda abroad against Republican Spain. And it actually happened that in those days the reactionary and fascist press abroad wrote about 'chaos' in Catalonia, and about a 'rebellion of the people against the Soviet dictatorship.' At the same time the insurgent radio transmitters in Salamanca and Saragossa broadcast unceasingly day and night orders couched in the same terms as those of the POUM: 'Hold your rifles ready, do not give up the fight at any price, combine with your brothers at the front, throw the Russian dictators out of your country.' "[77]

The Communist interpretation of the events was so well propagandized that, years later, the ingenuous Claude Bowers, U.S. ambassador to Spain, who during the Civil War was stationed in Hendaye, France, on the Franco-Spanish border, gave the following version: "In early May, the loyalist government moved against [the anarchists] with cold steel. A crisis had been provoked by the anarchists and the POUM, which was composed of Trotsky communists. It was generally believed that many of these were Franco agents. In factories, they were urging the seizure of private property and strikes to slow down production in the midst of war."[78]

The continuance of serious fighting on Wednesday, 5 May, brought the CNT leaders to the Generalitat Palace at an early hour. "The firing continues," wrote *Fragua Social*, the CNT organ in Valencia. "The streets of Barcelona are bathed in blood. The danger that our rear might crumble increases from hour to hour."[79]

"As the morning advanced," *Solidaridad Obrera* reported, "the fighting continued in various districts of the city and became general in the Plaza de Cataluña [where the telephone exchange was located], in the Calle de Clarís, Layetana [renamed Vía Durruti, where Casa CNT-FAI and the general commissariat of public order were uncomfortably close neighbors], and in the vicinity of the Generalitat Palace and the Avenida del 14 de Abril, increasing the number of wounded. . . . In several places . . . groups of individuals who could be described as *agents provocateurs* . . . devoted their time to firing their weapons and to arresting peaceful citizens, taking their union cards away from them. . . . One of the most lamentable activities of the *agents provocateurs* . . . [was sniping from housetops] in order to spread alarm in those districts where calm prevailed."[80]

On arriving at the Generalitat Palace the CNT leaders insisted that no time be lost in forming the new government. They were aware that Caballero could not hold out much longer against his adversaries and that, failing a settlement through mediation, he would be forced to implement the measures he had approved under duress the previous day. "Our efforts were unavailing," said the CNT, "for at 11:30 the session was adjourned. . . . When we reconvened, the Communists . . . argued that the [new government] should not be formed for three hours. We were [still] deliberating when we were informed that the central government had decided to take over public order and defense[81]. . . . We clearly observed the veiled satisfaction with which everyone welcomed the government's decision."[82] Furthermore, the *Boletín de Información* of the CNT and FAI alleged: "Companys and Tarradellas, as well as the UGT [PSUC] representatives, did everything possible to delay all the negotiations, so that the fighting would continue. Their pleasure could be seen whenever the fratricidal struggle increased in intensity and, on the other hand, they looked dismayed whenever they noted any pacification."[83]

At noon, after a meeting lasting only thirty minutes, the central government issued a statement announcing the public order and military decrees approved the previous day.[84] Colonel Antonio Escobar of the national republican guard was named delegate of public order, while General Sebastián Pozas was made military commander of the region—officially the Fourth Organic Division—and of the so-called Eastern Army in neighboring Aragon, where the CNT and FAI were dominant. These appointments nullified the Catalan councils of defense and internal security and, along with them, the cherished autonomy of the region.

Although, at its party congress held in June 1937, the Esquerra criticized Valencia for not responding immediately to the Catalan government's requests for reinforcements and denounced the delay as a "manuever" to force Catalonia to surrender her autonomy,[85] none of its leaders protested at the time. Indeed, the tone of the official announcement by the Generalitat Palace suggests that President Companys and the other Esquerra leaders accepted Valencia's decision with relief and that their fear of the CNT loomed larger at the time than their devotion to the autonomy of the region. "[The] government of the Republic, on its own initiative, has taken charge of public order in Catalonia," ran the announcement. "With resources superior to those available to the Generalitat, the government of the Republic can meet the needs of the present situation. This is no time for comment. All we can recommend and should recommend, if we wish to serve the interests of the war against fascism, is loyal and determined collaboration with the government of the Republic. Long live the Republic! . . . We urge everyone to lay down his arms and to end the turmoil in the streets."[86]

To be sure, Companys—like Premier Taradellas—would have preferred a gradual erosion of anarchist power to any impingement on Catalan autonomy, but once the fighting had erupted and his requests for reinforcements had been denied, he bowed without protest to Valencia's decision to assume control of public order. Haunted by the fear that he would be held accountable before history for the surrender of Catalan autonomy—a fear that became an obsession in later months[87]—Companys made numerous attempts after the power of the CNT and FAI had been broken to regain control of public order, but always without success.[88]

Until the May events, the faith of the anarchosyndicalist leadership in Companys had been virtually unquestioning. "In all his words and in all his actions," wrote Abad de Santillán, "there was but a single attitude, a moral and spiritual purpose, that we shared almost completely. There were few republicans who had acquired such a perfect understanding of the situation created on 19 July and there were few who expressed themselves with such clarity and such force in favor of a new social regime controlled by the workers. . . . The May events suddenly presented him to us in a different light. From that time on we began to doubt the sincerity of the president's past conduct. Was he or was he not implicated in the provocation of the bloody events? . . . While we played all our cards in an attempt to end that fratricidal bloodletting, we lacked the support of Companys for the first time since the July days. . . . Companys should explain to the Catalan working class, which supported him in very difficult times, if his role was that of an accomplice or of a prisoner in the May provocation and the subsequent invasion of the autonomous region."[89]

In accordance with the CNT's proposal of Tuesday night, a provisional government was finally set up on Wednesday, composed of four councillors: Carlos Martí Feced of the Esquerra, Valerio Mas, the secretary of the CNT Regional Committee, Antonio Sesé, the secretary general of the PSUC-controlled Catalan UGT, and Joaquín Pou of the Unió de Rabassaires. Although the question of Artemio Aiguadé's removal from the council of internal security was automatically resolved as a result of the taking over of public order by Valencia, Rodríguez Salas remained in charge of the general commissariat, pending the arrival of Antonio Escobar, the delegate of public order appointed by Valencia.

Fresh appeals were now broadcast from the Generalitat Palace. CNT secretary Mariano Vázquez again begged the workers to leave the streets. "We tell you that this situation must end. . . . We do not want this stigma to fall upon the Spanish anarchists. . . . This is not the moment, in front of piled-up corpses, to discuss who is right. It is essential that you disappear with your weapons from the streets. . . . We must not wait for others to do so. We must do so ourselves. Afterward we shall talk. If you decide, when you discuss our conduct at our next assembly, that we deserve to be shot, then you may shoot us, but now you must obey our slogans."[90] But Vázquez's stentorian lungs could not prevail against the aroused rank and file, and the struggle continued unabated.

Two incidents exacerbated the situation: Antonio Sesé, the newly designated PSUC-UGT councillor, was shot and killed when proceeding to the Generalitat Palace.[91] Who was responsible was never known, although accusations were plentiful. "It was alleged that he had been fired on from the [CNT] Public Entertainments Union," said the national committee of the CNT, "[but] it was subsequently proved that the bullet that cost him his life was not fired from the union building."[92] The Communists charged that he had been assassinated by "Trotskyist aggressors in the service of fascism,"[93] while Agustín Souchy, the CNT-FAI spokesman, declared that the shot had been fired "from a barricade belonging to Sesé's own party comrades."[94] That same day, Colonel Escobar, the newly appointed delegate of public order, was seriously wounded, when shot at on his arrival in Barcelona to occupy his new post.[95] As a result, Valencia named Lieutenant Colonel Alberto Arrando as the new delegate of public order.[96]

Up to now the only armed forces to arrive in Barcelona from Valencia were the marines dispatched by Indalecio Prieto on board the destroyers *Lepanto* and *Sánchez Barcaiztegui* to evacuate the president, but they were unable to reach the Catalan Parliament building.[97] Azaña was beside himself, furious over the "glacial indifference" and "insolent behavior" of Largo Caballero, and fearful of "perishing unjustly and tragically in Barcelona."[98]

In a telegraphed message to Prieto on Wednesday morning, complaining that for forty-eight hours he had not been able to discharge his presidential functions, he threatened to make a decision of "incalculable consequences" unless the government remedied the situation, and he told Prieto to give his message to Martínez Barrio, the speaker of the Cortes.[99] This was an obvious threat to resign, one of several made during the war, but never carried out owing largely to the efforts of Prieto, who, although contemptuous of the president's faintheartedness, valued him most highly as a constitutional cover for the Revolution.[100]

This was not the first time that Prieto had witnessed Azaña's faintheartedness. In October 1936, when the president was urging the government to leave Madrid,[101] he asked Prieto, "Does the government want the fascists to catch me here?" Irritated by Azaña's hurry to depart and by his concern over his personal safety, Prieto remarked to air force chief Hidalgo de Cisneros, "That cowardly fairy is acting like a hysterical whore."[102] Known as one of the most eloquent orators of the Republic, Prieto also had a reputation for vulgar language in private conversation.

"Prieto was very alarmed, seriously concerned," Azaña noted in his diary. "He did what he could to help me, but, even so, he did not quite understand the situation. The proof is that he told me that very morning that, in the government's opinion, *it was advisable that I leave for Valencia.* . . . 'The problem,' I said, 'is not that I am against going to Valencia, but that I cannot go into the street.' Martínez Barrio went to the telegraph and read the tape. It made such an impression upon him that, without waiting for the end of the conversation, he rushed off to see Caballero. He quickly returned, saying the government was going to do this, that, and the other, and I should be calm. I answered appropriately, and there was no further discussion."[103]

On Thursday morning, during a break in the fighting, the commander of the *Lepanto*, accompanied by five or six marines, presented himself in the Parliament building.[104] Azaña thought that any attempt to depart would be foolhardy. "Prieto continued to press me to take advantage of ten minutes of calm to leave for the port,"[105] but none of his suggestions appeared feasible to the president. "There was a faint smile of skepticism on Prieto's face," writes Zugazagoitia, a Prieto intimate and later minister of the interior. "He was sure that with a little courage any of his suggestions could be carried out successfully, preferably evacuation by sea. The distance from the Catalan Parliament building to the port was very short, and the journey could have been made by car in four minutes. But Don Manuel preferred four days of fears and insecurity to four minutes of resolution."[106] Finally, according to Azaña, after another conversation with Prieto, "more pressing than ever, during which he expressed the thought that perhaps I was balking at taking the risk, I decided to go." But just as he was about to leave the Parliament building, Azaña relates, the fighting resumed "with greater violence than ever," causing him to postpone his departure for Valencia until the following day.[107]

Meanwhile, it was clear from the heavy fighting on Wednesday that the calls for a cease-fire had not met with the unanimous approval of the rank and file. "Fighting had already been going on for three days," wrote Souchy, "and there was no sign of peace. . . . At about 5 P.M., the Regional Committee of the CNT made the following proposals: 'Hostilities to cease. Every party to keep its positions. The police and the civilians fighting on its side are asked to agree to a truce!' "[108] But these proposals passed unheeded.

The Friends of Durruti brought out a fresh leaflet: "A revolutionary junta has been formed in Barcelona. All elements responsible for the subversive assault maneuvering under cover of the government must be shot. The POUM must be admitted to the revolutionary junta because it has placed itself on the side of the workers."[109] The revolutionary junta, however, was never formed.[110] The regional committees of the CNT and FAI denounced the Friends of Durruti as *agents provocateurs* and declared that the leaflet was "absolutely intolerable and in conflict with the policy of the libertarian movement. . . . Everybody must fulfill the slogans of these committees. Now that the Council of the Generalitat has been formed, everybody must accept its decisions inasmuch as everybody is represented in it. All arms must leave the streets."[111]

"One more terrible blow against the embattled workers," wrote Felix Morrow, the Trotskyist critic of the POUM already quoted. "The regional committee of the CNT gave to the entire press . . . a denunciation of the Friends of Durruti as *agents provocateurs*. . . . The POUM press did not defend the left-wing anarchists against this foul slander."[112] The fact that the Friends of Durruti had publicly proposed that the POUM be admitted to the revolutionary junta was undoubtedly embarrassing to the POUM leadership, the more so as a rumor was in the air that the entire responsibility for the events was to be placed at the party's door. "I dimly foresaw," wrote George Orwell, "that when the fighting ended the entire blame would be laid upon the POUM, which was the weakest party and therefore the most suitable scapegoat."[113]

At about 8:30 Wednesday evening the provisional government appealed to "all the workers and people of Catalonia to lay down their arms and to forget their rancor and their enmities."[114] Other appeals were made. "Do not listen to the aggressors, to the Trotskyists who want the struggle to continue," the PSUC declared. "Let us unite around the government of the Generalitat."[115] Miguel Valdés, the PSUC leader, exhorted: "Workers of Barcelona, comrades of the CNT, we must not waste our energies a moment longer. We must put an end to the Trotskyist criminals, who in their newspapers continue inciting the antifascists of Catalonia to kill one another."[116]

Jacinto Toryho, the director of *Solidaridad Obrera*, an FAI member, also spoke. Referring to the "wave of collective insanity" that was destroying all the achievements of the first ten months of the Revolution as well as the "hope of the international proletariat," he stated: "This behavior, comrades of the CNT and UGT, comrades of the PSUC and FAI, comrades of the assault and national republican guards, is unbelievable; it is despicable, despicable because it is degrading to all of us. . . . In Barcelona the workers are assassinating one another. . . . This state of insanity that has transformed the most sensible people into madmen must end. . . . Just think that there is a front nearby. Just think that this front may become demoralized if it should learn of this hecatomb. . . . Comrades of the police, return to your barracks! Comrades of the CNT, return to your locals! Comrades of the PSUC and UGT, return to your centers! Let peace return!"[117]

Throughout the evening a joint appeal of the CNT and UGT was broadcast urging the workers to return to work. "It is necessary to return to normality. To continue this industrial inactivity at the present time when we are waging a war against fascism is equivalent to collaborating with our common enemy."[118]

As a result of these appeals, the fighting abated early Thursday morning, 6 May. Disconcerted by the attitude of their leaders, the anarchosyndicalists' ardor had begun to wane and many of them abandoned the barricades. But, as the morning advanced, fighting flared up again. The national committee of the CNT said:

The transport union ordered a return to work, but as the tracks were damaged, the repair cars had to be sent out before the streetcars could leave their depots. During the morning they had to return because they were fired upon. . . . The metro had to suspend its service because at some entrances the Communist police and members of Estat Catalá surrounded the passengers. . . . In some places large numbers of CNT cards were torn up. In others, our comrades were attacked. Our locals were besieged. . . . In the afternoon . . . the situation was more serious than ever. The comrades were ready to take matters into their own hands regardless of the consequences. [But] in spite of the many provocations . . . we could not close our eyes and wage the final battle. [It was perfectly clear] that we had played our enemies' game. They wanted us to go into the street; they wanted public order to pass into the hands of the [central] government. . . . We understood only too well the tragedy of those comrades who had been provoked and cornered and who had seen their comrades and friends fall. But, above all, it was necessary to prevent the entire struggle of the Spanish proletariat since 19 July from being suddenly reduced to naught.[119]

The POUM, feeling that further resistance was useless, instructed its followers to leave the barricades and presented the situation as optimistically as it could. "In view of the fact that the counterrevolutionary maneuver has been repulsed," declared the executive in a statement published in *La Batalla* on Thursday morning, 6 May, "the workers should withdraw from the struggle and return to work today, without fail and with discipline, to continue laboring with enthusiasm for the rapid defeat of fascism. The POUM orders all its armed militants to withdraw from the barricades and from the streets and to resume work, but to maintain a vigilant attitude." At the same time, La Batalla claimed that the proletariat had "obtained an important partial victory. . . . It has smashed the counterrevolutionary provocation. It has brought about the removal of those directly responsible for the provocation. It has dealt a serious blow to the bourgeoisie and the reformists. It could have achieved more, very much more, if the leaders of the predominant working-class organizations in Catalonia had risen to the occasion as did the workers. On the repeated orders of their leaders the masses have begun to withdraw from the struggle thus evidencing a great spirit of discipline. Nevertheless, the proletariat should remain vigilant. It should stand guard, bearing arms. It should keep watch over the activities of the bourgeoisie and the reformists and be ready to thwart their counterrevolutionary maneuvers." And a few days later, after the fighting had ended, the party's central committee declared: "As the workers fighting in the streets lacked concrete aims and responsible leadership, the POUM had no alternative but to organize and direct a strategic retreat, . . . avoiding a desperate action that might have degenerated into a 'putsch' and resulted in the complete destruction of the most advanced section of the proletariat. The experience of the 'May days' shows unequivocally that the only progressive solution to the present problem lies in the seizure of power by the working class and that it is therefore essential to coordinate the revolutionary activity of the working masses through the formation of a revolutionary workers' front, uniting all organizations ready to fight for the total destruction of fascism. This can be accomplished only through military victory at the front and the victory of the revolution in the rear. The central committee considers that the policy pursued by the party during the events was absolutely correct and fully endorses the line of the executive committee, convinced that it has defended the interests of the Revolution and the broad working masses."[120]

On Thursday evening, 6 May, news was received in Casa CNT-FAI that fifteen hundred assault guards had reached the outskirts of Tortosa, one hundred miles south of Barcelona. Both Federica Montseny, the CNT minister of health, who had arrived the previous day to help terminate the fighting, and Mariano Vázquez, the CNT secretary, hurried to the Generalitat Palace to communicate with Valencia. Not without reason were they apprehensive lest the assault guards en route to Barcelona might provoke every anarchist-controlled community in their path to insurrection. It fell to García Oliver, the CNT minister of justice, now back in Valencia, and to Angel Galarza, Largo Caballero's minister of the interior, to persuade Vázquez and Montseny to facilitate the passage of the assault guards through Catalonia and to restore peace to the embattled city before the arrival of reinforcements. The secret discussions that took place by teletypewriter to put an end to the fighting form part of Companys's notes and documents on the May events,[121] the essential portions of which are reproduced here:

[García Oliver]: This is the ministry of the interior, Valencia. Is the minister of health there?

[Montseny]: Yes . . . Listen García, Mariano is going to speak to you and then we shall talk to Galarza. . . .

[Vázquez]: This morning it looked as though the situation would soon clear up. . . . At midday, the situation began to deteriorate, because the police were preparing to attack union buildings. . . . The fact that Arrando [the new delegate of public order, who had replaced the wounded Escobar] has retained Rodríguez Salas as police commissioner has had a decisive influence on the situation. He is still in charge of the police and has no doubt instructed them to assume the attitude they are adopting. In many places the tearing up of CNT membership cards has been systematic. . . . Five comrades belonging to the bodyguard of Eroles [Dionisio Eroles, the anarchist chief of services, in the general commissariat of public order] have been taken from their homes and murdered. As a result of these and similar occurrences the comrades have taken steps to defend themselves. The atmosphere became more tense when news was received that 1,500 guards had arrived at Tortosa. It is impossible to foresee at this time what is going to happen. . . . [If] there is not a rapid change in the attitude of the police and in their leadership it will be impossible to prevent the fighting from becoming general again. . . . The impression should not be created that reprisals are going to be taken against [our] organization and militants. . . . If the police coming from Valencia continue to advance, it will be impossible to avoid flareups in the villages through which they have to pass and where there has been no trouble up to now.

[García Oliver]: This is García Oliver. . . . The minister of the interior has ordered the immediate dismissal of Rodríguez Salas. He is ready to resolve the situation in Catalonia in the fairest possible way. It is imperative that the assualt guards who are on their way to Barcelona reach their destination to relieve the police [who are] extremely exhausted, nervous and inflamed by the conflict. . . . You must understand this and make it clear to the committees and comrades. It is also imperative that you make it clear to the comrades and villages through which these impartial, absolutely impartial forces of appeasement have to pass. [The] government knows that without this strict impartiality the conflict, far from being resolved, would become worse, and would spread to the whole of Catalonia and the rest of Spain, and would result in the government's political and military downfall. . . . [The] minister of the interior [is considering] the advisability of dispatching these forces by other means than by road, which is too long and full of [potential] obstacles that may be spread in their path by all those aggressors interested in prolonging the present situation in Barcelona and bringing about the collapse of the government. As the administration of public order has now been taken over, I repeat that it is advisable that you immediately instruct the comrades in the villages not to place any obstacles in the way of these forces of appeasement. On the contrary, they should give them every kind of assistance and receive them with affection, because otherwise the danger exists . . . that if they are attacked en route they will become angered, as a result of which we should only have succeeded in transforming the problem of Catalonia into a national bonfire in which inevitably we would all be rapidly consumed. Above all, pay immediate attention to the province of Tarragona, where the POUM and the separatists [a reference to Estat Catalá] have many supporters, with the object of preventing them from mixing with [our] comrades and inciting them to armed resistance against the forces of public order. . . .

[Vázquez]: [Although we understand] the undeniable advantage of relieving the police in Barcelona, we should recognize that the problem here does not require the intervention of the police. The position is such that if they were merely to receive orders to return to their barracks for a few hours normality would return completely. It is imperative that the police should not attack or do anything at all for a period of three to four hours. This period would be sufficient to restore confidence as a result of which barricades would disappear and the police would abandon the buildings and places they occupy. . . .

[Galarza]: This is the minister of the interior. On learning at 7:30 P.M. that police commissioner Rodríguez Salas was still in command, I made the following statement [to Arrando], which I copy from the tape I have in front of me: "There should immediately be placed at the head of the administration of security a police commissioner, who is a member of the regular police corps, a man in whom you have more confidence; and the representatives of the unions and parties should stop intervening in public order." [Arrando] replied as follows: "I absolutely agree and shall obey your instructions immediately." . . . [Regarding] the time you require [to restore confidence], I have no objection to the following: At 10 P.M., the police will receive orders not to fire a single shot and to refrain from attacking any building. Only those forces necessary for vigilance will remain on the streets, but without searching for arms or making arrests for a period of three hours. You will undertake the responsibility of seeing that your people in the street and in [their] locals withdraw to their homes during this period and do not fire a single shot. I am going to issue these orders. Obviously, you understand that if they are not observed loyally by both sides nothing will be gained. The Premier is calling me. Wait a moment. . . . [Here] is García Oliver. . . .

[Montseny]: García, what Galarza says we can accept on condition that the truce is called tomorrow from 6 to 9 A.M., so as to give us time to organize a mass peace demonstration attended by the whole of Barcelona, and headed by the representatives of the organizations with their banners bound together. We shall suggest this to the UGT and are sure it will agree. . . . ·

[Galarza]: With regard to those three hours . . . I have no objection to their being between 6 and 9 A.M. As for the demonstration, provided there are no aggressors, it appears to me to be a very good idea, but I fear that these elements may take advantage of the general state of tension and that the demonstration may begin well but end badly. Perhaps it would be better to hold it on Sunday instead of tomorrow [Friday] and announce it in a joint statement of the two labor organizations. I am going to give orders to the police to observe the maximum prudence during the night. Leave it to me to see that after 9 A.M. tomorrow new and relaxed forces will be there with a person of my absolute confidence in command. [This was a reference to Lieutenant Colonel Emilio Torres Iglesias of the assault guards, who was appointed police chief of Barcelona].[122] . . .

[Montseny]: Very well, Galarza. . . . The truce may prove to be a salvation, but bear in mind that I do not know up to what point your orders will be obeyed if the same persons remain in charge of public order. . . .

[Galarza]: Tomorrow, other officers will be there.[123] . . . But keep this absolutely to yourself lest there be someone interested in repeating the Escobar incident. Tell your people that some of them should try withdrawing to their homes after midnight, and if, as I hope, nothing prevents them from doing so and everyone else does the same, then three hours will not be necessary tomorrow for this operation. It will be very easy to make the test. However, this implies such responsibility for me that I hope not only that I can rely upon your help, but that you will understand that this is the last attempt I can make at this type of solution. Do not announce any of these agreements over the air, but give them to your men of confidence in writing and with your signature. Does this sound all right to you?

[Montseny]: We shall endeavor to make a test at night, although we cannot promise anything owing to the difficulty of getting around at night and orienting [our] people personally. . . . Mariano asks me to tell you that we should agree on 6 A.M. to 9 A.M., as this will give us time to work and will be much easier.

In accordance with their understanding with Galarza, Vázquez and Montseny worked feverishly throughout the night to arrange the truce. "We informed the Catalan organization of the agreements we had reached," said the national committee of the CNT, "and ordered the comrades to prepare to withdraw at 6 A.M."[124] Furthermore, directives were sent to the villages and towns on the main road to Barcelona to allow the assault guards to proceed without hindrance. In Tortosa, where fighting had erupted on Tuesday,[125] the local CNT was instructed not to offer any resistance to the assault guards. "Our comrades acted accordingly," said *Solidaridad Obrera*, "thereby displaying their discipline and respect for the directives of the organization."[126]

In Barcelona, several hours before dawn on Friday, 7 May, there were signs that the ardor of the anarchosyndicalists had finally spent itself. A feeling that it would be futile to continue the struggle against the will of their leaders had overwhelmed them, and disillusionment was widespread. Many withdrew from the barricades and disappeared into the darkness. At dawn, the local committees of the CNT and UGT issued a joint appeal: "Comrades, everybody return to work!"[127]

That evening the assault guards from Valencia, accompanied by a force of carabineers sent by finance minister Juan Negrin, entered the city unopposed. Reinforcements, equipped with the latest weapons, continued to arrive by land and sea, and within a few days the number in the region was estimated at twelve thousand.[128]

The power of the anarchosyndicalists in Catalonia, the citadel of the Spanish libertarian movement, had now been broken. What would have appeared inconceivable a few months earlier, in the heyday of the CNT and FAI, had now become a reality and the most portentous victory of the Communists since the beginning of the Revolution.

Notes

1. *Solidaridad Obrera* (Barcelona), 29 Jan. 1937.
2. Ibid., 4 May 1937.
3. Speech, *Treball*, 2 June 1937.
4. Luis Companys, "Notes and Documents on the Fighting in Barcelona, 3–7 May 1937," see chapter 27, n. 155.
5. *Por qué perdimos la guerra*, 133.
6. *Solidaridad Obrera* (Barcelona), 4 May 1937; Manuel Cruells, *Mayo sangriento*, 48. Cruells was a staff reporter in May 1937 on the *Diari de Barcelona*.
7. The official Communist history of the Civil War claims that Aiguadé was given authority to occupy the telephone exchange during a meeting of the Generalitat government "despite anarchist opposition" (*Guerra y revolución en España, 1936–1939*, III, 72). On the other hand, the CNT claimed that everyone in the government agreed that "Aiguadé had overstepped his authority" (report on the May events by the national committee of the CNT, *Cultura Proletaria*, 19 June 1937). See also *Boletín de Información* (CNT national committee), 24 June 1937; *Solidaridad Obrera*, 12 May 1937 (report by regional committees of the CNT, FAI, and Libertarian Youth). Furthermore, President Azaña states, apparently on the evidence of Tarradellas, that Aiguadé did not inform the other councillors of his decision (*Obras completas*, IV, 576).
8. See chapter 9, text to n. 113.
9. Azaña, *Obras*, IV, 576.
10. Ibid., IV, 577.
11. CNT national committee report, *Cultura Proletaria*, 19 June 1937.
12. *La CNT en la revolución española*, II, 192. Felipe Ubach, an aide to Premier Tarradellas, told me after the war that the premier was opposed to the raid on the *telefónica*, but nevertheless sided with Companys during the cabinet debate out of loyalty to the president.
13. Cruells, 55–56.
14. *Cultura Proletaria*, 12 June 1937.
15. *Homage to Catalonia*, 169.
16. *La Batalla* (Barcelona), 4 May 1937.
17. After the cessation of hostilities the CNT defense committee in Sans released four hundred national republican guards, whom it had arrested at the inception of the fighting (see *Solidaridad Obrera* [Barcelona], 9 May 1937).
18. *La revolución y la guerra en España*, 144. President Azaña records: "All the working-class suburbs were in the hands of the rebels. The Generalitat, the departments of the interior and finance, etcetera, etcetera, were besieged" (*Obras*, IV, 579).
19. Interview, *Fragua Social*, 15 May 1937.
20. Evidence from Cándido Bolívar, when interviewed by me after the war.
21. CNT national committee report, *Cultura Proletaria*, 19 June 1937.
22. *Obras*, IV, 577–78. Jaume Miravittles, a member of the Esquerra, who accompanied Tarradellas on his hazardous trip through Barcelona to the parliament building to see Azaña writes: "The interview with Azaña was painful. We found a man physically and morally destroyed" (*Episodis de la guerra civil espanyola*, 148).
23. *Obras*, IV, 578.
24. *Caníbales políticos*, 69–70.
25. Companys, "Notes and Documents." The date of the telephone conversation is given erroneously as Tuesday, 7 May, instead of Tuesday, 4 May.

26. Orwell, 174–75.

27. No attempt is made in this chapter to provide a detailed account of the street fighting. Firsthand reports can be found in the following: *La Batalla* (Barcelona), *Boletín de Información, CNT-FAI, Catalunya, El Día Gráfico, Las Noticias, El Noticiero Universal, La Publicitat, Solidaridad Obrera* (Barcelona), *Treball, Ultima Hora, La Vanguardia* (all of which were published almost every day during the events); Abad de Santillán, *Por qué perdimos la guerra*; Cruells; Marcel Ollivier, *Les journées sanglantes de Barcelone*; Orwell; Agustín Souchy [Bauer], *La verdad sobre los sucesos en la retaguardia leal.*

28. Interview, *Fragua Social*, 15 May 1937.

29. *La revolución*, 147.

30. As given in Rudolf Rocker, *Extranjeros en España*, 130; see also Souchy, *La verdad*, 19.

31. See *Caníbales políticos*, 70.

32. Statement made to Charles Orr, editor of the *Spanish Revolution*, English-language bulletin of the POUM (quoted in Felix Morrow, *Revolution and Counter-Revolution in Spain*, 100).

33. Orwell, 208.

34. 4 May 1937.

35. CNT national committee report, *Cultura Proletaria*, 19 June 1937.

36. Ibid.

37. Ibid.

38. Both Carlos Hernández Zancajo and Mariano Muñoz Sánchez, it may be recalled, were appointed by Largo Caballero in February 1937 to scrutinize the work of officers and commissars of every rank (see chapter 25, text to nn. 19 and 20).

39. Companys, "Notes and Documents."

40. Ibid. Under the provisions of the statute, Madrid was empowered to take control of internal order in Catalonia if the interests of the state were threatened.

41. Ibid.

42. A copy of this document was loaned to me by Jordi Arquer, to whom I am indebted for much scrupulous research. A typewritten copy is deposited in the Bolloten Collection, Hoover Institution, Stanford. The Spanish Communists were obviously unaware of the existence of this document when they published a glowing tribute to Aiguadé in their refugee newspaper, *España Popular*, on 7 Dec. 1946.

43. Prieto, *Palabras al viento*, 203.

44. Statement to me by Cisneros, when interviewed after the war.

45. Information given to me by Constancia de la Mora, the wife of air force chief Hidalgo de Cisneros. The messages were read by her in the navy and air ministry and are probably those referred to in n. 103, below.

46. *Obras*, IV, 580.

47. *La Vanguardia*, 5 May 1937.

48. *La verdad*, 19.

49. 4 May 1937.

50. National committee report, *Cultura Proletaria*, 19 June 1937.

51. Ibid.

52. *Solidaridad Obrera* (Barcelona), 5 May 1937.

53. Ibid.

54. *Cultura Proletaria*, 12 June 1937.

55. *Ensayo crítico sobre la revolución española*, 23–24.

56. National committee report, *Cultura Proletaria*, 19 June 1937.

57. *La Voz Valenciana*, 5 May 1937.

58. Companys, "Notes and Documents."

59. Statement issued by national committee of the CNT, published in *Fragua Social*, 7 May 1937.

60. *Fragua Social*, 15 May 1937.

61. For an account by the Trotskyists, Clara and Paul Thalmann, both members of the Bolshevik Leninists, of the efforts by Moulin, one of their most active militants, to influence Jaime Balius, the vice-secretary of the Friends of Durruti, "in all-night discussions," to abandon his "innate anarchist mistrust of the Marxists" and to collaborate with the Trotskyists, see *Revolution für die Freiheit*, 189–90.

62. As given in Morrow, *Revolution*, 82; see also Orwell, 207.

63. As reproduced in *La Batalla* (Barcelona), 6 May 1937. See also Fenner Brockway, *Truth about Barcelona*, 10; Morrow, *Revolution*, 82; G. Munis, *Jalones de derrota*, 305; Orwell, 207.

64. 6 May 1937. See also *Treball*, 6 May 1937, for the PSUC's criticism of *La Batalla*.

65. There is no record in any of the newspapers of the period of any appeal over the radio by POUM leaders for a cease-fire.

66. See text to n. 34, above.

67. 19 May 1937.

68. This appears to be a reference to the conference held on the night of 3 May (see text to n. 24).

69. *Revolution*, 94, and footnote.

70. *Vanguard*, Feb. 1939.

71. *IV International*, 1 June 1937.

72. *Service d'Information et de Presse por la Quatrième Internationale*, June 1937.

73. *Unser Wort*, mid-March 1939.

74. Speech on 9 May 1937, as given in Díaz, *Tres años de lucha*, 432. This speech is quoted more fully at the beginning of chapter 29.

75. 9 May 1937.

76. 10 May 1937. See also his article in *Labour Monthly*, Aug. 1937.

77. *International Press Correspondence*, 11 Nov. 1937.

78. *My Mission to Spain*, 356.

79. Editorial, reviewing events, 14 May 1937.

80. 6 May 1937.

81. According to Companys, the news that the government had taken over public order was received at 12:30 P.M. ("Notes and Documents").

82. National committee report, *Cultura Proletaria*, 19 June 1937.

83. 21 May 1937, as given in Souchy, *La verdad*, 59.

84. *La Correspondencia de Valencia* (evening newspaper), 5 May 1937.

85. *El Día Gráfico*, 15 June 1937.

86. *La Vanguardia*, 6 May 1937.

87. According to Miguel Serra Pamies, a member of the PSUC's central committee and councillor in the Generalitat government after the May events (personal interview after the war, when he had ceased to be a member of the party).

88. Within a few days after the fighting had ended and the region had been occupied by twelve thousand assault guards, Companys expressed the hope in an interview given to *Ce Soir* (Paris) that the administration of public order would be returned to the region (as given in *Hoja Oficial del Lunes*, 17 May 1937).

89. *La revolución*, 148–50.

90. *Solidaridad Obrera* (Barcelona), 6 May 1937.

91. He was replaced by Rafael Vidiella, the PSUC-UGT leader.

92. *Cultura Proletaria*, 19 June 1937.

93. *Frente Rojo*, 6 May 1938. See also speech by Rafael Vidiella, ibid., 4 June 1938.

94. *La Verdad*, 30–31.

95. *El Noticiero Universal*, 6 May 1937.

96. *El Día Gráfico*, 6 May 1937.

97. Azaña, *Obras*, IV, 580–81.

98. Ibid., 585, 587.

99. Ibid., 581.

100. See chapter 9, text to n. 114.

101. See his remarks to Largo Caballero, chapter 9, text to n. 119.

102. According to information given to me by Cisneros.

103. *Obras*, IV, 581. The tapes of the frequent messages exchanged between Prieto and Azaña during the fighting have been preserved by the Servicio Histórico Militar of Madrid. Ramón Salas Larrazábal, *Historia del ejército popular de la república*, I, 1027, states that from a reading of the tapes Azaña appears "fearful, cowardly, and supplicatory." This appriasal I have been able to verify thanks to the courtesy of José Clavería Prenafeta of the Servicio Histórico Militar, who provided me with a microfilm copy. The tapes are published, in part, by Colonel José Manuel Martínez Bande, *La invasión de Aragón y el desembarco en Mallorca*, 282–92. My copy is with the Bolloten Collection, Archives, Hoover Institution, Stanford.

104. *Obras*, IV, 584.

105. Ibid., 585.

106. *Historia de la guerra en España*, 255–56.

107. *Obras*, IV, 585–88.

108. *La verdad*, 24.

109. As given in Cruells, 70.

110. This was confirmed to me by Jaime Balius, vice-secretary of the Friends of Durruti (see his letter dated 24 June 1946 in file "Amigos of Durruti," Bolloten Collection, Archives, Hoover Institution, Stanford).

111. *Solidaridad Obrera* (Barcelona), 6 May 1937.

112. Morrow, *Revolution*, 95.

113. Orwell, 183–84.

114. *El Noticiero Universal*, 6 May 1937.

115. *El Día Gráfico*, 6 May 1937.

116. *El Noticiero Universal*, 6 May 1937.

117. *Solidaridad Obrera* (Barcelona), 6 May 1937.

118. *El Noticiero Universal*, 6 May 1937.

119. *Cultura Proletaria*, 19 June 1937.

120. *La Batalla* (Barcelona), 13 May 1937.

121. See chapter 27, n. 155. The date of the document is given erroneously as Tuesday, 7 May, but it is obvious from internal evidence that the date should have been Thursday, 6 May.

122. See *La Publicitat*, 8 May 1937. Torres was regarded as being friendly to the CNT and FAI (Abad de Santillán, *Por qué perdimos la guerra*, 136; Victor Alba, *El marxismo en España, 1919–1939*, II, 448; R. Louzon, *La contra-revolución en España*, 123, n. 6; Salas Larrazábal, I, 1039–40). At all events, he was replaced a few weeks later, after the fall of the Largo Caballero government, by Lieutenant Colonel Ricardo Burillo, a Communist party member and former police chief of Madrid.

123. The appointments made by Galarza, published in the *Gaceta de la República*, 11 May 1937, were as follows: José Echevarría Novoa, delegate of public order; Emilio Torres Iglesias, police chief of Barcelona; José María Díaz de Ceballos, general commissioner of security (as given in *Solidaridad Obrera* [Barcelona], 12 May 1937).

124. *Cultura Proletaria*, 19 June 1937.

125. *Solidaridad Obrera* (Barcelona), 16 May 1937; *Treball*, 14 May 1937; also Companys, "Notes and Documents," and Cruells, 89.

126. 16 May 1937.

127. *Solidaridad Obrera* (Barcelona), 7 May 1937.

128. Barcelona correspondent, *Times*, 12 May 1937. *Solidaridad Obrera* (Barcelona), 9 May 1937, reported that five thousand assault guards arrived on the evening of 7 May.

Scenes in Barcelona May 7th 1937 after the barricades had been abandoned by the workers.

4

The Counter Revolution on the March

MASSACRE OF WORKERS AT TARRAGONA

On Wednesday , May 5th, at 8am, a large force of police suddenly appeared at the Central Telephone Exchange of Tarragona, plentifully armed with weapons and grenades for taking it by assault. They occupied it without encountering any resistance whatever from the workers. Once masters of the building, they took control of the urban and inter-urban communications, cutting the lines of the working class and anarchist organisations.

Four hours later, a conference took place at the general military headquarters between Comrade Casanovas, representing the telephone workers, and the lieutenant-colonel, chief of coastal military forces, when a detailed account of the unexpected developments was given. As a result of the conference, it was agreed that the police forces should be withdrawn from the first floor, where the apparatus was, and should keep watch in the vestibule.

But fifteen minutes later the Chief of the Police announced that the Commissar for Public Order in Taragona refused to carry out the agreement, following very strict orders received from Barcelona.

While these conferences and telephonic conversations were proceeding, our comrades discovered activity on a large scale in the local headquarters of the Republican Esquerra, numerous individuals entering without arms and leaving with a gun. The same thing happened, but with less cynicism, in the headquarters of the Socialist Party and in the People's Club.

The following day, in the morning, a violent and open attack on our organisation began. Supported by intense musketry fire and launched against the quarters of the Libertarian Youth. This attack was repulsed. In face of the gravity of such aggression, we appointed a commission to get in touch with the Commissioner of the Catalonian Government with a view to demanding a general conference of all the anti-fascist forces in order to avoid a repetition of such lamentable episodes. He agreed to this request and called together the representatives of all the political and industrial organisations.

In order to acquaint themselves with what was happening at Tarragona, our comrades Castello and Rueda had set out for that town. On arriving, they heard a lively fusillade and realised that it had to do with a fresh assault on the headquarters of the Libertarian Youth led by a part of the State forces, collaborating with elements from different organisations. The tremendous violence of the attack made it possible for the assailants this time to achieve their aim.

At the conference there were the representatives of the Republican Esquerra, the UGT, the United Socialist Party, besides the various military authorities and those of the Catalonian Government.

During the conference, the delegate of the Central Government, the Air Force Captain Barbeta, disclosed that he had explicit instructions from the government to use every kind of force — *including the air force* — to destroy the syndicalist and anarchist organisation if it did not surrender its arms.

(*Solidaridad Obrera*)
(*Spain and the World*, 19th July 1937)

MURDER AND PROVOCATION IN TORTOSA

Nowhere in Catalonia reigned more cordial understanding between the leaders of the CNT and the UGT than in Tortosa. All difficulties of collective order which might arise in towns or villages were resolved by the representatives of the two organisations with the best of good-will. So much so that despite the fact that communal meetings for May 1st had been banned in Catalonia, all efforts were made by the comrades of Tortosa to make it possible to hold meetings in their region. Thus one imagined that the occurrences in Barcelona would result in bloody repercussions in Tortosa.

Now this is what happened:

On the Wednesday of the tragic week, in the early hours of the morning, the commander of the Republican National Guard of Tortosa, Lieutenant-Colonel Domenech, at the head of fifty guards, captured the Telephonic Central, after having forced an entrance, and took possession of the offices as well as control of communications.

Whereupon, a commission made up of comrades of the CNT came to discuss matters with the police chief. An agreement was reached according to which the police should withdraw from the building and end their provocative disposition, which in fact they did.

Calm was thus restored once more, but was to last only a short time. By nightfall, elements of the public forces, mingling with individuals belonging to different parties, began to fire in the darkness on our comrades, who, fearing an attack were patrolling the streets. Firing was taken up everywhere, but our comrades soon dominated the insurgents, and tranquility was once more restored. The guards who had provoked this conflict were made prisoners; not only were their lives respected, but all their needs were attended to.

The situation was restored to normal, when news came that some few kilometres from the town were armed forces from Valencia and that, according to official orders of the Regional Committee of the CNT they should be allowed free passage. Our comrades respected this request. But their loyalty was not respected. Once the Valencia forces entered the town they arrested all those who carried with them the CNT card.

At the same time, as if we had only to expect such a thing to happen, numerous armed individuals came out of the local headquarters of the UGT and other parties, and began to carry out searches and arrests, so that in a very short time confusion and disorder had reached alarming proportions. As to the governmental forces, instead of establishing order once more, they joined the rebels, soon putting the quiet and hard working town of Tortosa at the mercy of a few individuals.

Pillaging then began. The homes of members of the CNT were attacked, the invaders taking possession of all the money, clothes and food which they found in them.

Not content with that, they eventually left for the nearby villages where they continued to loot, above all in the peasants' collectives of the CNT. In one of the villages through which they passed, Tivenys, they issued an order demanding that all properties which had been requisitoned must be returned, right away, to their original owners. Naturally, no one took this seriously, but it certainly shows the seditious ideology of these people.

The prisons in Tortosa were soon full; not much time would be wasted in emptying them.

In fact, during the night of June 6th, an individual known as 'Chaparro', with a few men belonging to his gang, accompanied by an assault guard whose name we do not know, went to the dungeons of the Town Hall where some twenty comrades were detained in company with a corporal of the assault guards who had been arrested because he had refused to fire on the workers. On the pretext of taking them to a tribune of enquiry, they were all made to come out, amongst them being the above mentioned corporal named Bebrer, besides Antonio Odena and the well known militant Rogelio Tena. They were all taken in the direction of Tarragona, chained together and under escort. Of what happened to them later, we cannot say other than the fact that they were found in Tarragona, but reduced to corpses, thrown in the gutter like dogs.

(Solidaridad Obrera)

(Spain and the World, 19th July 1937)

VILLAGES AND COLLECTIVES RUTHLESSLY ATTACKED

MARSA — On the 3rd of June a number of Guards invaded the region, searched the homes of militant workers of the CNT, assaulted the headquarters of the Confederation and destroyed its banner. During the course of conversations with the inhabitants of the town, the Guards recognised the legality of the CNT Collectives, but among them were a number of 'uncontrollables' who had to be eliminated. In order to justify their arrest of various comrades, they spread the rumour that the militants of the CNT had drawn up a list of workers whom they were going to kill.

MORA DE EBRO — A large number of Assault Guards came to this town on June 5th, with lorries and tanks, and installed themselves in the headquarters of the PSUC. They immediately arrested fourteen comrades of the Executive Committee of the Collective, of the Union and of the Municipal Council. On the 7th, they returned to seize the headquarters of the Collective, converting it into an office for their own use. They launched themselves into a systematic campaign of persecution against the workers, many being arrested at their work. The authorities who were acting in this manner then proceeded to declare the Collective dissolved and non-existent, and restored the land to its former owners, all of whom are hostile to the present regime. The result of this campaign is that *more than 300 families were left without means of obtaining a livelihood*; in other words, these counter-revolutionists effected the complete economic ruin of the town. Not satisfied with this, they published a manifesto calling upon all those who felt that they had suffered any losses through the May events to declare themselves. Only three persons presented themselves: Juan Pinol, José Campos, and José Montagut. The first was the mayor of the town under the dictatorship, the second, president of the Radical Party, and the third, one of the former political bosses. Because of the accusations of these three individuals, 21 comrades were arrested and taken to Tarragona.

AMPOSTA — On June 5th, the Guards came and arrested all the members of the CNT in the Municipal Buildings as well as members of the Collectives. There was an immediate protest on the part of the town, everybody laying down his work to a man.

GARCIA REUS — The Guards invaded the town asking for the president of the Collective. Comrade Francisco Montserrat introduced himself, and the official in charge of the forces, after asking him several questions, ended by declaring the Collective dissolved and sealing their general warehouse, which had formerly belonged to one José Luisnella, ex-chief of the Civil Guards during the period of Primo de Rivera. Later, all the grain of the Collective was sequestered, together with all the other property of the Collective, the entire thing being put at the disposal of the Municipal Authorities. One farm was excepted. It was returned to its former owner. The following comrades were arrested and taken to Falcet: Francisco Montserrat, Domench Bargallo, Solè, Carreres, Angers, Mani, Bartolomi, Pascual and Escoda.

MAS DE TONI — The Guards descended upon the town with a great display of force. Openly threatening the workers of the Collective, they ordered them to surrender their arms. The workers had none.

They became particularly vicious with the political delegate, pretending that they intended to shoot him. They forced him to get into a car, telling him that they were taking him to Lèrida, but upon arriving at Vergoz they made him get out. When he finally walked back to Mas de Toni again, he found that the Guards had robbed the town of all its possessions, taking both money and foodstuffs.

CERVERA — The reaction reached extreme limits in this locality of Lèrida. An expedition of Assault and National Guards came to the town on June 11th under the command of Captain Santa Cruz. The first act was to break into the headquarters of the CNT and destroy their radio. The homes of a number of members of the CNT were searched. On the 12th, more Guards arrived under the command of Captain Montorò, who promised to behave properly. But the promise was forgotten soon enough. A child of twelve years was going home from a boy's school with his mother, both of them refugees from Madrid. A Guard, seeing a CNT insignia upon the child's clothing, tore it off violently and grossly insulted both of them while doing it. Then there began a regime of occupation. They sacked the residence of a hospital delegate and stole forty pairs of pants that had been manufactured in a collectivised workshop for the patients in the hospital.

(*Spain and the World*, 22nd September 1937)

THE CAMPAIGN AGAINST POUM

At the beginning of the war, the Communist Press began to speak of Trotskyism in its international aspect. Nobody was concerned about the question. A little later, the same papers were saying that Spain also had Trotskyites and pointed to their presence in the POUM. Still later, they said that this whole Party was tied up to Trotskyism, and then, in the face of the freedom from bias among the political and social elements, the same dailies began to say that the Trotskyites were in the service of the Gestapo and constituted an advance guard of fascism in our camp. To develop their campaign they refused to recognise the fact that the POUM had thousands of fighters in the front lines, where they were fighting as courageously as any other Spanish anti-fascists. To accuse this Party of Trotskyism, they ignored the attacks that it was constantly receiving from the Bulletin of the Fourth International, attached to Trotsky. They forgot all good faith, all loyalty in words and acts, in order to unleash a campaign against the POUM that no other powerful organisation would have tolerated.

This is a very serious problem and we must express our opinion about it. We must begin by saying that the political position of the POUM is very similar to that maintained by the Communist Party in Spain up to a short time ago. It is enough to take this into consideration to realise that we, the workers of the CNT, are not very much in agreement with the ideology of the POUM. It will also be worth while recalling that this Party has attacked our Organisation many times before the 19th of July, and since then. We have no obligation towards them, and therefore our words must have more value now.

In the campaign against the POUM, we see a break in the wall erected by all the anti-fascist organisations in Spain. We therefore regard this as extraordinarily grave. We must declare with full emphasis that this is playing with fire and paying attention to foreign interests rather than to the needs of our own country. The persecutions cannot meet with the approval of anybody who is free of sectarianism, and must shock great numbers of revolutionary workers. And truly terrible consequences for all of us can follow from this shock. The danger for all of us who are concerned with the war and the Revolution is great enough without allowing ourselves to abandon the firm ground of reason.

But even more, we workers of the CNT see in this campaign an example of reactionary effrontery. If in the past they have fought only against the POUM, they will now fight also against the CNT, as well as against members of the UGT who refuse to submit to foreign influences and want to create the social and political conditions that are indispensible for our victory. We see that they do not take into consideration the work of those who are now the object of the most unjustifiable attacks. Largo Caballero, Pascual Tomas, Ricardo Zabalza, Carlos Rubiera, Baràibar and other men with great prestige among the workers are beginning fought in a campaign as dishonourable as it is furious, by the same elements who are conducting the persecutions against the POUM.

We can expect anything from this offensive. We repeat: *Anything*. Precisely for this reason we shout out our warning to the Spanish proletariat. We shall never grow tired of repeating that we must all have a greater sense of responsibility. But neither can we pass over in silence what we loyally and sincerely interpret as one of the most serious attacks against the Revolution, against the liberties of the people, and against the spirit of harmony that we have been forging during the past eleven months of struggle against fascism. But we shall be vigilant and watchful. We cannot tolerate rivalries whose merits are highly debatable, are foreign to our interests, and endanger our anti-fascist victory.

(*Solidaridad Obrera*)
(*Spain and the World*, 19th July 1937)

5

Political Persecution in Republican Spain
Emma Goldman

On my first visit to Spain in September 1936, nothing surprised me
so much as the amount of political freedom I found everywhere.
True it did not extend to fascists; but outside of these deliberate
enemies of the revolution and the emancipation of the workers in
Spain, everyone of the anti-fascist front enjoyed political freedom
which hardly existed in any of the so called European
democracies. The one party that made the utmost use of this was
the PSUC, the Stalinist party in revolutionary Spain. Their radio
and loudspeakers filled the air. Their daily marches in military
formation with their flags waving were flaunted in everybody's
face. They seemed to take a special pleasure in marching past the
House of the Regional Committee as if they wanted to make the
CNT-FAI aware of their determination to strike the blow when
they will attain to complete power. This was obvious to anyone
among the foreign delegates and comrades who had come to help
in the anti-fascist struggle. Not so our Spanish comrades. They
made light of the communist brazenness. They insisted that this
circus clap trap could not decide the revolutionary struggle, and
that they themselves had more important things to do than waste
their time in idle display. It seemed to me that the Spanish
comrades had little understanding of mass psychology which needs
flagwagging, speeches, music and demonstrations — that while the
CNT-FAI however, were concentrated on their constructive tasks,
and fighting on the various fronts, their communist allies made hay
while their sun shone. They have since proved that they knew what
they were about.

During my stay of three months I visited many of the

collectivised estates and factories, maternities and hospitals in Barcelona, and last but not least, also the 'Modelo' prison. This is the place that had harboured some of the most distinguished revolutionaries and anarchists of Catalonia. Our own heroic comrades Durruti and Ascaso, García Oliver and many others had been cell neighbours of Companys, the new President of the Generalitat. I visited this institution in the presence of a comrade, a physician who had made a special study of criminal psychology. The director gave me free access to every part of the prison, and the right to speak to any of the fascists without the presence of guards. Among the few hundred admirers of Franco were officers and priests. They assured me in one voice of the decent and just treatment they were receiving from the management in charge of the place, most of whom were CNT-FAI men.

The possibility that fascists would soon be replaced by revolutionists and anarchists was far removed from my mind. If anything, the high water mark of the revolution in the autumn of 1936 held out hopes that the stain of prison would be wiped out once Franco and his hordes were defeated.

The report of the foul murder of the most gentle of anarchists, Camillo Berneri and his room mate, the anarchist Barbieri, was followed by wholesale arrests, mutilation and death. They seemed too fantastic, the change in the internal political situation too incredible to be true. I decided to go back to Spain to see for myself how far the new found freedom of the Spanish masses had been annihilated by Stalin's henchmen.

Once again I arrived on the 16th September this year. I went straight to Valencia and there discovered that 1,500 CNT members, comrades of the FAI and the Libertarian Youth, hundreds of the POUM and even members of the International Brigade were filling the prisons of Valencia. During my short stay there I left no stone unturned to get permission to visit some of our comrades, among them Gustel Dorster whom I had known in Germany as most active in the anarcho-syndicalist movement before Hitler ascended to power. I was assured that I would be given permission; but at the last moment, before my return to Barcelona, I was informed that foreigners were not allowed to see the prison. I soon discovered the same situation repeated in every town and village I visited. Thousands of comrades and other genuine revolutionaries were filling the prisons under the Negrin-Prieto and Stalinist regime.

When I came back to Barcelona in the early part of October, I immediately sought to see our comrades in the Modelo prison. After many difficulties, comrade Augustin Souchy succeeded in obtaining permission to have an interview with a few of the German comrades. Much to my surprise I found on my arrival there that the same Director was still in charge. He too recognised me and he again gave me full entry to the prison. I did not need to speak to the comrades through the hideous bars. I was in the hall where they foregather, surrounded by German, Italian, Bulgarian, Russian and Spanish comrades, all trying to speak at once and tell me of their conditions. I discovered that no charge whatever that would stand in any Court, even under capitalism, had been preferred against them, except the idiotic charge of 'Trotskyism'.

These men from every part of the globe had flocked to Spain, often begging their way across, to help the Spanish Revolution, to join the ranks of the anti-fascists, and to lay down their lives in the struggle against Franco were held captive. Others again had been picked up on the street and had vanished without leaving any trace behind. Among the many was Reis, son of the internationally known Russian Menshevik Abramovich.

The most recent victim is Kurt Landau, a former member of the Executive Committee of the Austrian Communist Party, and before his arrest on the Executive Committee of the POUM. Every effort to find him has met with failure. In view of the disappearance of Andres Nin of the POUM and scores of others it is reasonable to conclude that Kurt Landau met with the same fate.

But to return to the Modelo prison. It is impossible to give all the names, because there are so many incarcerated there. The most outstanding is a comrade who, in a high responsible position before the May events, had turned over millions of pesetas to the Generalitat found in Churches and Palaces. He is held under the ludicrous charge of having embezzled 100,000 pesetas.

Another one is comrade Helmut Klose, a member of the CNT-FAI. He was arrested on the 2nd July. No charge has been made up to this date, neither was he brought before a Judge. Comrade Klose was a member of the FAUD in Germany (German anarcho-syndicalist organisation). After having been arrested several times, he emigrated to Yugoslavia in the summer of 1933. Expelled from there in February 1937, because of anti-fascist activity. He came to Spain in March. He joined the frontier service of the FAI, in the 'De la Costa' battalion. After the dissolution of this battalion, in June he took his discharge, and entered the service of the agricultural collective of San Anores. In compliance with the request from his group he later undertook the reorganisation of the Tailors' Collective of the Emigrants Committee. The charge made by the Cheka of his having disarmed officers while in the Frontier Service at Figueras is entirely without foundation.

Commander de Albert Kille. He was arrested on September 7th. No reason was given. In Germany he had belonged since 1919 to the Productive Supply Union. Besides this he was a member of the Communist Party. In 1933 he emigrated to Austria. After the February events he fled to Prague: but later returned to Austria, whence he was expelled and left for France. Here he joined the German anarcho-syndicalist group. In August 1936, he went to Spain, where he at once proceeded to the front. He was wounded once. He belonged to the Durruti column right up to the time of the militarisation. In June he took his discharge.

I also visited the POUM Sector. Many of these prisoners are Spaniards, but among them there are also a large number of foreigners, Italian, French, Russian and German. Two members of the POUM approached me personally. They said little of their own suffering, but begged me to take a message to their own wives in Paris. They were Nicolas Sundelevich — the son of the famous Menshevik who had spent the longest part of his life in Siberia. Nicolas Sundelevich certainly did not give me the impression of being guilty of the serious charges made against him of 'having given the fascists information' among the many other charges against him. It takes the perverted communist mind to hold a man in prison because in 1922 he had illegally left Russia.

Richard Tietz was arrested as he came out of the Argentine Consulate in Barcelona where he had gone on behalf of his wife, previously arrested. When he demanded to know the grounds of his arrest the Commissar nonchalantly said "I consider it just". That was evidently enough to keep Richard Tietz in the Modelo since July.

As far as prison conditions can be humane the Modelo is certainly superior to the cheka prisons introduced in Spain by the Stalinists according to the best party examples of Soviet Russia. The 'Modelo' still maintains its traditional political privileges such as the right of the inmates to freely mingle together, organise their committees to represent them with the director, receiving parcels, tobacco, etc., in addition to the scanty prison fare. They can also write and receive letters and reading material. Besides, the prisoners issue little prison papers and bulletins which they can paste in the corridors where they all foregather. Both in the section of our comrades and the POUM I found such prison papers, posters and photographs of the heroes of the two parties. The POUM had even a very fine drawing of Andres Nin and a picture of Rosa Luxemburg, while the anarchist's side had Ascaso and Durruti on their wall.

Most interesting was the Durruti cell which he had occupied in Barcelona until released by the 1936 elections. It was left intact as it had been while Durruti was its involuntary lodger. Several large posters of our gallant comrade made the cell very much alive. The strangest part is however, that the Durruti cell is in the fascist section. In answer to my question as to how Durruti's cell comes to be in there, I was told by the guard "as an example of the living spirit of Durruti that will destroy fascism". I wanted very much to have the Durruti cell photographed, but permission had to be obtained from the Minister of Justice. I gave up the idea. I had never in my life asked favours of Ministers of Justice, much less would I ask for anything from the counter-revolutionary government, the Spanish Cheka.

My next visit was to the womens' prison, which I found better kept and more cheerful than the Modelo. Only six women politicals were there at the time. Among them Katia Landau the wife of Kurt Landau, who had been arrested several months before him. She was like the old time Russian revolutionists, utterly devoted to her ideas. I already knew of her husband's disappearance and possible end; but I did not have the heart to disclose this fact to her. This was in October. In November I was informed by some of her comrades in Paris that Mrs Landau had begun a hunger strike on the 11th November. I have just received word that as a result of two hunger strikes Katia Landau has been released.

A few days before my departure from Spain I was informed on good authority that the old dreadful Bastille — Montjuich — was again being used to house political prisoners. The infamous Montjuich, whose every stone could tell of man's inhumanity to man, of the thousands put to death by the most savage methods of torture, or driven mad or to suicide. Montjuich, where in 1897 the

Spanish Inquisition had been reintroduced by Canova Del Castillo, then Premier of Spain. It was at his behest that 300 workers, among them distinguished Spanish anarchists, had been kept for months in underground damp and dirty cells — repeatedly tortured and denied counsel. It was in Montjuich that Francisco Ferrer was murdered by the Spanish Government and the Catholic Church. Last year I visited this terrifying fortress. Then it held no prisoners. The cells were empty. We descended into black depths with torches guiding our way. I almost seemed to hear the agonised cries of the thousands of victims who had breathed their last in the ghastly holes. It was a relief to get into the light again.

History does repeat itself after all. Montjuich again serves its old ghastly purpose. It is overcrowded with ardent revolutionaries who had been among the first to rush to the various fronts. Militias of the Durruti column freely giving their health and strength but unwilling to be turned into military automatoms — members of the International Brigade who had come to Spain from every land to fight fascism, only to discover the harsh differentiation against them, their officers and the political commissars, and the criminal waste of human lives due to the military ignorance and for party purpose and glory. All these and more are incarcerated in the fortress of Montjuich.

Since the world slaughter and the continued horror under dictatorship, red and black, human sensibilities have been atrophied; but there must be a few left who still have a sense of justice. True Anatole France, Georg Brandes and so many great souls whose protests saved twenty two victims of the Soviet State in 1922 are no longer with us. Still there are the Gides, the Silones, Aldous Huxley, Havelock Ellis, John Cowper Powys, Rebecca West, Ethel Mannin and others, who would surely protest if made aware of the political persecutions rampant under the Negrín, Prieto and Communist regime.

At any rate I cannot be silent in the face of such barbarous political persecutions. In justice to the thousands of our comrades in prison I have left behind, I will, and must, speak out.

London, December 1937
(*Spain and the World*, 10th December 1937)

6
Biographical Epilogue (1987)

I. Contributors to this volume

JOSÉ PEIRATS (b.1908) was active in the young libertarian and anarchist groups at an early age at the time of the Primo de Rivera dictatorship in the 1920s. In the civil was was a member of the 26th Division (formerly Durruti column) from 1937 until the end of the war though he opposed both the entry of the CNT-FAI in the government and the militarisation of the militias. In *The Anarchists in the Spanish Revolution* (1977) he expresses thoughts and reflections which have no place in the vocabulary of those academic historians who can only distinguish between success and failure.

Among [the anarchists of the CNT-FAI], were some whose refusal to compromise cannot be lightly dismissed. For them the only solution was to leave an indelible mark on the present without compromising the future of the organization. The indelible marks they made — constructive revolutionary experiments like the collectives, artistic and cultural achievements, new models of free, communal living — can survive the most ferocious counterrevolution. Acting positively without compromising the future of the organization meant staying out of intrigues, avoiding complicity with the counterrevolution within the government, protecting the organization and its militants from the vainglory of rulers or the pride of the newly rich. It meant avoiding contacts with a petty world of petty appetites in favour of a future as vast and eternal as space and time, in which all of us will be judged by our deeds, and not by the cleverness of our explanations and justifications.

Two things have to be distinguished in a revolution: the constructive work of changing peoples' minds and economic circumstances, which is the result of an incorruptible integrity; and the historical outcome of the revolution itself. It is not always possible to control the fate of a political revolution, which has its own laws of rise and decline. But we can see to it that when the revolution is over there remain concrete, constructive achievements. Perhaps this residue of permanent achievement is the only real and useful revolution.

Pity the revolution that devours itself in order to obtain victory. Pity the revolution that waits for a final triumph to put its ideals into practice. In spite of all the difficulties and deceptions, the Spanish revolution had the good fortune to come to full fruition. The revolutionary work of the collectives will be an indelible mark in time and space.

The rest will pass into history like a bad dream. So too will pass into oblivion those who, remembering with pleasure their positions as ministers and their military commands, are still thinking, twenty years later[9], about an impossible kind of libertarian political party. The real Spanish libertarian movement has historical, psychological, and popular roots that go deep. When uprooted, the movement dies.

From a distance of more than 20 years, I believe that those of us who consistently opposed collaboration with the government had as our only alternative a principled, heroic defeat. I believe there was an unavowed complicity among many militants who were enemies of participation and who were self-righteously angry while they permitted the participation to take place. And yet they were sincere in their own way, sincere in their powerlessness. They could offer no solution that would simultaneously preserve so many precious things: victory in the war against fascism, progress in the revolution, complete loyalty to their ideas, and the preservation of their own lives. Lacking the power to perform miracles, these men consoled themselves by clinging to their principles.

AUGUSTIN SOUCHY (1892-1984) was in charge of the foreign propaganda for the CNT-FAI from 1936-39. He was a lifelong anarcho-syndicalist and less of an anarchist. He supported the 1939-45 war and with Rudolf Rocker advocated the participation of anarchists in local council elections in post-war Germany. His account of the May Days is probably the only detailed account ever published. It was, as far as this writer can recollect, first published in SPAIN AND THE WORLD as a Supplement in June 1937 and thereafter by the CNT-FAI Propaganda Section in Barcelona in English, French and Spanish versions as pamphlets. The version published here does not include Souchy's reflections and conjectures as to the consequences of the defeat. The uniqueness and importance of this document as it stands is that its author, as he reveals in his Memoirs, kept an hour by hour diary of the events as they unfolded and was throughout in the Casa CNT-FAI which was at the centre of the struggle. However it should be said that Souchy supported the compromising role of the CNT-FAI leadership, and later that year (10th November 1937) we published in SPAIN AND THE WORLD an interview with him (to be published in full in the main centenary volume[10]) in which he confirmed that while he was convinced at the time and still was that our comrades could have won the day 'for a certain period' he was 'completely convinced that the CNT was right to stop the war at all costs' in spite of the fact that he also admitted that once the struggle had ended 'we hoped for a united front, fraternally renewed with peace and tolerance between all anti-fascist sections. Unfortunately things turned out completely differently'.

BURNETT BOLLOTEN (b.1908) was a United Press correspondent in Spain during the Civil War who has since devoted all his energies to establishing the facts of that social upheaval in which he, unlike the academic historians who were, and still are, being conned by communist propaganda into accepting the myth of communist efficiency, recognised the overriding importance of the social revolution — 'far reaching...more profound in some respects than the Bolshevik Revolution in its early stages'. And from his wide study of the literature on the subject he concluded that 'millions of discerning people outside Spain were kept in ignorance, not only of its depth and range, but even of its existence, by virtue of a policy of duplicity and dissimulation of which there is no parallel in history'. That was in 1961 when the first edition of his History was published. That year too Hugh Thomas' *History* was published and in France Broué and Temime's *La revolution et la guerre d'Espagne*[11]. Thomas' *History* got all the attention from his academic colleagues, and not very long after Bolloten's book disappeared. It resurfaced with another publisher in 1968 and again disappeared until in 1979 an enlarged edition was published by The University of North Carolina Press who in kindly giving FREEDOM PRESS permission to reprint Chapter 28 Barcelona: The May Events, gave us the welcome news that 'within the next year or so' they will be publishing a new edition of Burnett Bolloten's History with the title *The Spanish Civil War: Revolution and Counter-revolution.*

SPAIN AND THE WORLD was a four page anarchist newspaper published fortnightly from December 1936 to December 1938 (47 issues) and from February 1939 to June 3rd 1939 six issues appeared with the title *Revolt! Incorporating Spain and the World.* As well as the Centenary Series Volume of Reprints this journal is available on microfilm.

II. Historians and Communist Propaganda

One cannot take either Thomas or Joll seriously when in spite of new editions of their works which should surely allow for greater accuracy on vital issues they persist in presenting the incident that sparked off the armed struggle on May 3rd as 'In the afternoon on May 3, the chief of the police in Barcelona, Eusebio Rodriguez Salas, went to the Telefonica, and visited the censor's department on the first floor intent on taking over the building' (*Thomas* p.654). ...'the trouble began with the arrival of the socialist chief of police to investigate suspicions that the CNT were tapping lines for their own purposes (*Joll* p.252). Gabriel Jackson is a little bit more adventurous when he writes that Salas 'intended, peaceably, he hoped, but by force if necessary, to take control of the Barcelona telephone central. He arrived with a company of Assault guards and was met by fire from within the building'. [Surely only an academic could suggest that in the middle of a Civil war when the situation was so tense that the normal May Day celebrations in Barcelona were cancelled that the chief of police could go to the Telefonica with a company of Assault guards and hope to take control 'peaceably'!]

The most recent Communist version in *Spain Against Fascism 1936-39*[12] manages to get every detail wrong. 'On May 2, the forces of public order under the command of a major presented themselves at the Barcelona telephone exchange, which was occupied by the FAI, and attempted to take it over' (p21). A valuable source book, probably long out of print, is *Communism & the Spanish Civil War* by David Cattell (University of California Press 1955) at the time Assistant Professor of Political Science at the University (yes, a good academic!). In the chapter on the May Crisis the opening paragraph sums up the situation:

The culmination of the Communist purge of the revolutionary Left came in May 1937. A crisis had slowly developed throughout March and April of 1937. The Cheka terror had aroused the anger of all the Anarchists and the POUM, and the growing severity of the attacks had alarmed many of them for the safety of the whole revolutionary Left (p.141). Nevertheless the Professor does not get all his facts quite right. He writes: "The CNT had been in control of the Telephone Exchange Building...since the first days of the revolt and all efforts by the Generalitat to dislodge it had been futile."

First of all there was joint control by the two Unions CNT-UGT and secondly the Collectivization Decree of October 1936 had made workers control of the Telefonica perfectly legal. He is only half right when he says that 'as a result the CNT had complete control over almost all telephone communications in Catalonia' because the UGT also shared the control. He then states that on May 3, the Director of Public Security, Rodrigues Salas of the PSUC, 'sent a police patrol to relieve the CNT of control of the building which it refused to do voluntarily. This was the spark igniting an outbreak of hostilities all over Barcelona.' (p.142)

The facts of the armed attack on the Telefonica are beyond dispute from contemporary sources. Why then all these accounts if not because it suits the writers' and parties' particular approaches. In case the reader has not spotted the omission in both Thomas' and Joll's accounts: they have conveniently left out, to quote Bolloten, 'the three truckloads of assault guards' that accompanied Salas the Chief of Police thus converting a provocative action into a visit ('Salas went to the Telefonica, and visited the censor's department'). The academics who got it all wrong — when the non academics like Bolloten, Cruells, Peirats, Morrow got it right — are reluctant to admit it and so long as they are in control they continue to peddle their misinformation.

The Communists are in quite a different category. They have no concern whatsoever for the truth as they demonstrated so clearly by their propaganda throughout the Civil War. However in this interlude of New Look communism it is difficult to understand why they published *Cockburn in Spain*[13] for the 50th anniversary of the military uprising which met not with a rallying call by the Popular Front government — only too anxious to make a deal with Franco — but by resistance of the anonymous workers and the revolutionary organisations. This collection of dispatches by

Cockburn (alias 'Frank Pitcairn') to the *Daily Worker* deserves to be read by the generation for whom the civil war is history in order to understand what another generation, who were defending the revolution in Spain, had to contend with from the Communist propaganda machine liberally subsidised by Stalin's Russia. This volume includes two dispatches on the May Days. 'Pitcairn Lifts Barcelona Veil' — Trotskyist Rising as Signal' were the headlines in the *Daily Worker* of May 11 and a few choice samples from the man Graham Greene, no less, has described as one of 'the two greatest journalists of the twentieth century' (the other being G.K. Chesterton):

"...what was being prepared was a situation in which the Italian and German governments could land troops or marines quite openly on the Catalan coasts, declaring that they were doing so 'in order to preserve order'.

That was the aim. Probably that is still the aim. The instrument for all this lay ready to hand for the Germans and Italians in the shape of the Trotskyist organisation known as the POUM.

The POUM, acting in cooperation with well-known criminal elements, and with certain other deluded persons in the anarchist organisations, planned, organised and led the attack in the rearguard, accurately timed to coincide with the attack on the Bilbao front.

In the past the leaders of the POUM have frequently sought to deny their complicity as agents of a Fascist cause against the People's Front. This time they are convicted out of their own mouths as clearly as their allies, operating in the Soviet Union, who confessed to the crimes of espionage, sabotage and attempted murder against the government of the Soviet Union."

"900 dead and 2500 wounded is the figure officially given by Diaz [Secretary of the Spanish Communist Party]...It was not, by any means the first of such attacks. Why was it, for instance, that at the moment of the big Italian drive at Guadalajara, the Trotskyists and their deluded anarchist friends attempted a similar rising in another district? Why was it that the same thing happened two months before at the time of the heavy Fascist attack at Jarama, when, while Spaniards and Englishmen, and honest anti-fascists of every nation in Europe, were being killed holding Arganda Bridge, the Trotskyist swine suddenly produced their arms 200 kilometres from the front and attacked the rear?"

James Pettifer, the editor of this revealing libel against the real revolutionaries in the Spanish struggle does not even have the intellectual honesty to point out that Trotsky and Trotskyists like Felix Morrow disowned the POUM, and that their 'allies operating in the Soviet Union etc.' were rehabilitated under Krutschev. Many more, according to the *Guardian*'s Moscow correspondent, including Trotsky, may find their 'rightful places' in Russian history books. Indeed Mr Pettifer omitted to mention the disappearance of Jose Diaz, referred to in Cockburn-Pitcairn's dispatch, and that of a number of top Russian officials in Barcelona at the time of the May Days in the Stalin purges. Suffice it to say *Cockburn in Spain* was advertised in *Marxism Today* but has not been reviewed, which is not surprising.

However the current official Communist Party view in this country is contained in Pamphlet 67 in the series aptly titled *OUR HISTORY* (my emphasis on the OUR). It is quite impossible to analyse this farrago in the space at my disposal. Obviously their approach to the May Days is influenced by their attitude to the struggle as a war against fascism and their involvement in the political intrigues, bearing in mind that at that time the Spanish Communist Party was of no significance without support from Moscow paid for with the Spanish Gold reserves.

The authors of this pamphlet both spent a year in Spain (after the May Days, but we are not told what they were doing there) and on the strength of their presence there we are assured that 'stories about "NKVD agents" in Spain, especially in relation to the fight against Trotskyism' is in their view 'apocryphal'. They maintain that they were 'sometimes in circumstances' [why not tell us what they were doing in Spain] 'in which we might reasonably have expected to hear of such activities by Soviet security agents if they had been at all widespread. We never did.' But what follows is equivocal to say the least: 'This is not proof, of course that they never existed' and they quote Santiago Carrillo to bear them out.

"Listen, I myself was a sort of Minister of the Interior, at Madrid, in the Junta of Defence. What I can tell you is that in the course of those two months I had no contact with services of the Soviet Union."

"Yes, but you are talking about 1936" said his interlocutor.

"Perhaps there were some later" replied Carrillo. "Perhaps there were some even then" and later in the interview he states "...It is true that it has been said that there were GPU prisons. I personally have no proof that there were and I never saw one, even though I believe the Soviet people must have had certain services in Spain, connected with the presence of their volunteers who were fighting at the front" (quoted by the authors from Santiago Carrillo *Dialogue on Spain* 1976).

One has to bear in mind that Carrillo was a minor figure in the CP during the Civil War and only since assumed prominence as leader of the Spanish Europo-Communist Party after Franco's death (Diaz having disappeared in the Stalinist purges and Hernandez having defected[14]), which explains why in his *Dialogue on Spain*[15] he permits himself reflections, which the CP hardliners will still not admit, when he told his interviewer:

"Now with the hindsight and the experience of history, it may be thought that if the overspill of the international contradictions of the Soviet revolutionary process into the international sphere could have been avoided, it might then have been possible to avoid at the same time the *putsch* of the Trotskyists and anarchists. But how was it possible to avoid that overspill when through its historical weight and the situation in those years, the Russian Revolution was the dominant factor in the entire revolutionary movement?"

If I have understood that last sentence I can only say that for this writer it makes no sense since within two months of the military uprising in July 1936 Moscow's instructions to the Spanish CP were to destroy the revolution and help to re-establish government authority in Spain, and especially in Catalonia where the social revolution had been most marked and where, of course, the communists were virtually non-existent.

Marxism Today[16] which can be full of surprises (partly, one suspects, in its struggle for circulation) let in a chink of light in the *Letters* page of its October 1985 issue about 'Reappraising Spain' which led one to hope that for the 50th anniversary of the Civil War *M.T.* would go to town. Jerry Kitchen, the writer of the letter, pointed out that in the previous issue an article had been published in *M.T.* highlighting

the mistaken position adopted by the British CP when it sought to defend the Moscow show trials [in 1936]. It also needs to be recognised that these trials coincided with the period in which Stalin sought to determine the outcome of events in Spain.

The decision taken by the Communists in Spain to purge the anarchists and the elimination of the POUM forces, culminating in the murder of Andres Nin, were all events inspired by Stalin.

The writer goes on to emphasise that he is a loyal member of the Party, but he thinks nevertheless that for the 50th anniversary 'British Communists are, surely, indebted critically to examine the official Soviet account of this period. If they do so the future of the British CP would be greatly enhanced.'

The July 1986 issue had Bob Geldof on the cover, pages of advertisements for books on the Civil War and a feature by Manuel Azcarate (son of the pro-Negrin socialist Ambassador in London at the time) who is a leading CPer in Spain today. It is too short (2 pages) to cover all the issues, which may explain why the anarchists are mentioned only once (and not as 'agents of Franco', or *putschists*). But it contains the most damning indictment of the role of the Communists that could be contained in a few paragraphs. He points out that only the USSR apart from Mexico, 'gave military help to the republic' (he doesn't mention that it was all paid for in gold) and that as a result it gave the Party great prestige. However 'after the shameful Munich agreement in which the Western democracies capitulated to Hitler, Stalin directed his efforts towards concluding a pact with Hitler, and Soviet aid to the Spanish republic subsequently declined considerably.' This is factually wrong. The Munich Pact was signed in September *1938* when to all intents and purposes the end of the military struggle was only a question of time. But Senor Azcarate goes on to consider

the other problem [concerning] the serious consequences of the Stalinist repression. 1936 was the year of the trials in which Stalin liquidated some of the best leaders of the Bolshevik revolution of 1917, to impose his implacable and dictatorial power. The Communist International imposed on all the parties, and naturally also on the Spanish party, the thesis that the Trotskyists were traitors and agents of fascism.

This had very negative consequences for the struggle of the Spanish people; repression was unleashed against the Trotskyists and serious divisions were created between Communists and other left forces, including trade unionists, anarchists and left Socialists. This weakened the struggle of the people.

In view of the foregoing how many more editions of the academic historians' Histories of the Civil War before they abandon the myth of the Communists' efficiency in the fight against Franco?

Paul Preston, one of the academics I had thought of as being enlightened, recently criticised Bolloten's account of the Communist Party's suppression of revolution 'in the interests of a conventional war effort and of Soviet foreign policy' in spite of his 'tenacious scholarship' because

it tends to be developed within an interpretative vacuum. Communist policy can be assessed seriously only in the light of its efficacy within the Republican war effort. By effectively concluding his story in May 1937, Bolloten permits himself to examine the dictatorial nature of Communist methods without having to assess the realism of their policies once they had gained the upper hand.[17]

Unlike the academics, Preston included apparently, Bolloten saw clearly that the resistance to the military uprising in July 1936 did not come from the government (which was prepared to make a deal with Franco) but from workers in the CNT and UGT, and the anarchists in the FAI, the dissident communists in the POUM and the CP which was small but also very revolutionary. As Brenan reminds us, when the Republic came in in 1931 'the Comintern was going through a period of Left extremism and the Communist party violently opposed all compromise with the bourgeois state'. And Brenan adds that 'it was left to the dissident Communist group (the "Trotskyists") under Maurin to advocate a democratic republic and a popular front'.[18] In 1934 the Communists even took part in the Asturian rising.

In a Special Spanish Number of Controversy (July 1937 Vol.1 No.10) Jon Kimche (then a member of the ILP, young and more revolutionary than he has since become) contributed an interesting article on 'Communists and Anarchists' which opens with these reminders to his fellow socialists — but which it would seem equally apply to historians such as Paul Preston:

Political memories are short. Misleading propaganda is rife within the Labour movement. It is necessary to refresh memories. What happened twelve months ago in Spain? Let Frank Pitcairn [alias Claud Coburn] and the Daily Worker [now Morning Star] speak:

A leading article in the *Daily Worker* three days after the revolt had broken out summed up the situation as follows:

"In Spain, Socialists and Communists fought shoulder to shoulder in armed battle to defend their Trade Unions and political organisations, to guard the Spanish Republic and to defend democratic liberties so that they could advance towards a *Spanish Soviet Republic*"

In the same issue Pitcairn reported that "Streets here are being patrolled by cars filled with armed workers who are preserving order and discipline. *Preparations are going forward for the organisation of a permanent workers' militia.*"

On July 23rd the streamer headline across the front page of the *Daily Worker* recounts how 'WORKERS' POWER SMASHED FASCISM'. A few days later Pitcairn was reporting from Lerida 'how the peasants and workers were taking control of everything and how as a result he found everywhere 'calm and confidence in the fight against Fascism'.

Kimche maintains that the Communist Party changed its policy in the early days of August 1936. On July 31 came the first reports of Italian intervention 'and almost simultaneously the emphasis of the Communist Party was changed from the workers' role in Spain to the Democratic republic in their stead' and the purpose of his documented article was not to show whether 'this was good or bad tactics' but to demonstrate 'that this change of policy of the Communist Party had to lead to the fratricidal struggle which raged over the whole of Catalonia for several days ten months later'.

Unlike Paul Preston who maintains that Communist policy can be assessed 'only in the light of its efficacy within the Republican war effort', I suggest that it can only be assessed in the light of *its efficacy as the principle instrument in the counter-revolution which led to the May Days and the final defeat of the social revolution in 1937 and the ignominious military defeat in 1939.* Such an assessment would certainly make the Communists qualify for Paul Preston's accolade as to the 'realism of their policies once they had gained the upper hand'. It is time the myth of Communist efficiency in Spain during the civil war was exorcised!

III. The POUM and Friends of Durruti
The POUM's case was given by Fenner Brockway in *The Truth*

About Barcelona[19] and by John McGovern, the catholic ILP member of Parliament, in *Terror in Spain*[20]. I regret that space considerations prevented me from including extracts from those pamphlets in the section dealing with the *Counter-revolution on the March*. But for the interested reader *Freedom Press Bookshop* can supply photocopies of these pamphlets.

George Orwell was attached to fighting units of the POUM and on leave in Barcelona during the May Days. Chapter 10 of *Homage to Catalonia*[21] describes his 'personal experiences'. I think its value now can be summed up by the opening paragraph:

About midday on 3 May a friend crossing the lounge of the hotel said casually: "There's been some kind of trouble at the Telephone Exchange, I hear." For some reason I paid no attention to it at the time.

Orwell really didn't know what was happening. One reads in the previous chapter that:

I had told everyone for a long time past that I was going to leave the P.O.U.M. As far as my purely personal preferences went I would have liked to join the Anarchists. If one became a member of the C.N.T. it was possible to enter the F.A.I. militia but I was told that the F.A.I. were likelier to send me to Teruel than to Madrid. If I wanted to go to Madrid I must join the International Column, which meant getting a recommendation from a member of the Communist Party.

So he sought out a Communist friend who said he could fix him up, and Orwell writes: 'If I had been in better health I should probably have agreed there and then'. However the next Chapter in which he deals with the May Days and the Communists' complicity is detailed and valuable.

The POUM was labelled 'Trotskyite' by the Communists and, apparently still is, in spite of the fact that the Old Man himself hadn't a good word to say for them in *The Lesson of Spain. The Last Warning!*[22]. But by far the most important Trotskyist contribution is Felix Morrow's *Revolution and Counter-Revolution in Spain*[23] a book much disliked by Communists, POUMists and some of my anarchist comrades because it attacks them all! It is an important book as, in its way, is the pro-CP Left Book Club *The Civil War in Spain* by Frank Jellinek. Both were writing as the blurb to Morrow's 1978 reprint puts it *in the white heat of the struggle*. Their allegiances and prejudices were there for all to see; but the result is exciting. Just as is Souchy's account of the May Days in this volume.

The Cahiers Mensuels *Spartacus* No 7 (probably 1937-38) published an excellent pamphlet by Marcel Ollivier *Les Journées sanglantes de Barcelone*. In 1979 No 110 *Chronique de la Revolution Espagnole* by H. Chazé of the Union Communiste 1933-1939 (a contemporary and admirer of Marie Louise Berneri and of her father Camillo Berneri who had a deep respect for the anarchist rank and file in Spain but was, as many anarchists were, critical of the leadership) is a collection of his writings during the Civil War worth re-reading.

I feel that anarchist historians should deal at greater length with *The Friends of Durruti*, mentioned briefly both in Souchy's and Bolloten's accounts of the May Days in Barcelona. Peirats explains the emergence of this 'extremist group' as a reaction to the CNT's 'policy of pacification [which] led to a deep disgust among the union fighters'. 'The higher committees of the CNT immediately disavowed this group' writes the CNT's historiographer who nevertheless considers that it 'never had the importance ascribed to it by some foreign historians'. The reasons for his conclusions are the 'relative unimportance of its members, POUM participation, and the Marxist flavour of some of its communiqués'.

A small volume edited by Miguel Pecina and Frank Mintz on *Los Amigos de Durruti, Los Trotsquistas y los Sucesos de Mayo* (Madrid, 1978) comprises what the editors consider to be 'the most representative texts and manifestos' issued by *Los Amigos*.

IV. Lessons

A serious academic work which includes a chapter on the May Days is David T. Cattell's *Communism and the Spanish Civil War*[24]. Compared with Hugh Thomas's summing up: 'The "May Days" of Barcelona showed that the anarchists could not be counted upon to respond as one to any situation: a gulf stretched between the anarchist ministers, busy trying to win the war, and the anarchist youth' David Cattell is on the contrary surprised by the

docile attitude on the part of the Anarchists...It certainly showed a restraint on their part which is unusual. Never before had the Anarchists shown such discipline to the decisions of their leaders.

Anarchists would probably not necessarily agree with Cattell's explanation for the rank and file anarchists wanting leadership. One would need to analyse the composition of the CNT after July 1936 when its membership and that of the UGT rocketed into millions, since all workers were required to join a Union. But at least he interpreted the situation — so well described by Souchy — whereas Thomas seems unable to present facts without his prejudices taking over.

I trust I shall be forgiven for including in this *Bibliographical Epilogue* a reference to my *Lessons of the Spanish Revolution* (Freedom Press 1953, 1972, 1983) in which four chapters deal directly or indirectly with the May Days, or for concluding with some reflections inspired by Malatesta's writings on the anarchist revolution. I wrote[25]

I do not propose to develop the insurrectionary argument here; it has already been clearly put by Malatesta. All I would add is that subsequent events have confirmed his arguments as well as his warnings. From the anarchist point of view obviously the Spanish Revolution of 1936-39 is the most significant social upheaval in our time. Though the anarchists have not yet subjected these events to the exhaustive analysis they deserve, the broad outline contained in the literature available could so easily be used to illustrate these pages of Malatesta's writings, just as his writings, because they foresaw the very problems that faced the anarchists and other revolutionaries in the Spanish struggle, could have served them as a tactical manual, the acceptance and application of which would have in all probability pushed the revolutionary possibilities to their fullest limits resulting either in the complete defeat of Franco's *coup d'etat* in the first weeks of the struggle or in his military victory in the first six months, but without the possibility of lording over the country.

In other words, if the anarchists and syndicalist "leaders" after the spectacular victories of the first days of the military rising had sought to exploit their richly deserved prestige in the eyes of the workers by directing all their energies and propaganda to the workers inciting them to enlarge and consolidate the revolutionary gains of the 19th July, rather than seeking to use that prestige to cement a unity at top level with the other organisations and parties (which is what they did with scant success) they would have liberated *all* the latent and potential revolutionary forces in the country and beyond their frontiers. This may have ended in defeat within a few weeks. But it would have been defeat when the revolutionary feelings and expectations were still high — and therefore when it was possible to continue the struggle by other means. Whereas in prolonging the struggle by sacrificing the revolution to the war of fronts, not only did the politicians, with the support of the revolutionary organisations ensure military defeat, but also ensured that a people subjected for more than two years to great material privations as well as growing political dissensions between the parties and workers' organisations, when it did finally concede victory to Franco and his backers, was exhausted, decimated, disillusioned, bitter and helpless. The great exodus of half a million Spaniards, who preferred exile and French concentration camps, to Spain under Franco, was no guarantee of continuity in the struggle, for they, no less than those left behind, and who escaped the repression, were also exhausted, disillusioned and...*divided*.

NOTES

Editor's Preface

1. Manuel Cruells. *Mayo Sangriento: Barcelona, 1937* (Barcelona Editorial Juventud 1970)
2. Hugh Thomas. *The Spanish Civil War* (London 1961, 1965, 1977)
3. Gabriel Jackson. *The Spanish Republic and the Civil War 1931-1939* (Princeton 1965)
4. James Joll. *The Anarchists* (London 1964, 1979)
5. George Woodcock. *Anarchism* (New York & London 1962, 1975, 1986)
6. Nan Green & A.M. Elliott. *Spain Against Fascism 1936-9* (London 1979?)
7. Burnett Bolloten. *The Spanish Revolution: The Left and the Struggle for Power during the Civil War* (Chapel Hill N. Carolina 1979)
8. José Peirats. *Anarchists in the Spanish Revolution* (Detroit 1977?)

I. Contributors to this Volume

9. The first version of Peirats was published in Italian by Edizioni RL Genoa 1962 with the title *Breve Storia del Sindicalismo Libertario Spagnolo* which explains the reference to 'twenty years later'. One could add that in 1977 when the English edition was published, of the three surviving 'anarchist' Ministers, Oliver was unrepentant, Montseny had some doubts, and Juan Lopez (who was an able syndicalist, a *Treintista* — the breakaway group from the CNT in 1931 with Pestana) returned to Spain in 1967 and accepted a Franco government post in the Valencia co-operatives.
10. *Spain & the World* Selections from that journal (1936-1939) Volume 2 in the FREEDOM PRESS Centenary Series 1987 of which the present volume is a Supplement.
11. Broué et Temime. *La Revolution et la Guerre d'Espagne* (Paris 1961). The English translation (London 1972) of this important history was unnoticed here and soon went out of print.

II. Historians and Communist Propaganda

12. See Note 6. This 32 page pamphlet is No 67 in the series *Our History* published by the 'History Group of the Communist Party' which 'exists to

forward the study of history from a Marxist standpoint'. To judge by this pamphlet this does not involve any concern with facts!

13. Claud Cockburn. *Cockburn in Spain* (Edited by James Pettifer) (London 1986)

14. Jesus Hernandez. *Yo Fui un Ministro de Stalin* (Mexico 1953). Hernandez was one of the top Spanish Communists in 1936. Moscow trained, he was a minister in both the Caballero and Negrin governments. After the defeat he spent four years in Russia and was a member of the Politburo. In 1943 went to Mexico and spilled the beans both about the Politburo and the Party's activities during the Civil War. No wonder *Our History* does not mention him.

15. Santiago Carrillo. *Dialogue on Spain* (London 1976)

16. *Marxism Today* Monthly published by the British Communist Party Vol 30 No 10 and Vol 31 No 7

17. Paul Preston (Ed). *Revolution & War in Spain 1931-1939* (London 1984) p7

18. Gerald Brenan. *The Spanish Labyrinth* (Cambridge 1943)

III. The POUM and the Counter-Revolution

19. Fenner Brockway. *The Truth About Barcelona* (London 1937). A 16-page pamphlet full of interesting facts mixed with the ILP/POUM propaganda. It includes a 2-page 'skeleton record of events' by John McNair and Jon Kimche who were in Barcelona at the time.

20. John McGovern MP *Terror in Spain: How the COMMUNIST INTERNATIONAL has destroyed Working Class Unity, undermined the fight against Franco and suppressed the Social Revolution* (London n.d. probably 1937 or early 1938)

21. George Orwell. *Homage to Catalonia* (London 1938)

22. published by J.R. Strachen. W.I.P. London 1938

23. London 1976. This edition includes The Civil War in Spain (1936) and Revolution & Counter-Revolution in Spain (1938) as well as a 10-page unsigned Foreword (March 1976).

IV. Lessons

24. Berkeley USA 1955. As the title of this book makes clear the author is mainly concerned with the role of the Communists, with the result that he provides an important documentation. His notes and bibliography are important.

25. *Malatesta Life and Ideas* Compiled and Edited by Vernon Richards (London, Freedom Press 1965) Malatesta's Relevance Today (Part III pp298-99)

*   *   *

Two books on Emma Goldman on the Spanish Revolution have appeared recently. *Vision on Fire* (New Paltz, NY 1983) ably 'Edited with Introductions by David Porter' and José Peirats'

Emma Goldman *Una Mujer en la Tormenta del Siglo* (Barcelona 1983). Emma was not in Spain during the May Days though she went on at least three occasions to Spain during the civil war, and was the London representative of the CNT-FAI. Above all she was a prolific letter writer copies of which were invariably sent to all her correspondents and admirers, especially in the USA, a no mean task in the pre-photocopying age. Emma Goldman was fundamentally opposed to all the compromises made by the CNT-FAI but as their representative in London and having to contend with the then powerful Communist propaganda machine, what she said in public was not always what she wrote in her letters to comrades. In the course of preparing this small volume comrade Frederico Arcos sent me a copy of a letter she addressed to Max Nettlau on May 9th 1937 which includes *inter alia* the following:

Now, while I am heart and soul with the struggle of the Spanish comrades, and while I have done my utmost to plead their cause, for which I would cheerfully give my life, I must insist that they are vulnerable: they have made terrible mistakes which are already bearing fruit. I hold Federica Montseny, Garcia Oliver and several others of the leading comrades responsible for the gains made by the communists and for the danger now threatening the Spanish Revolution and the CNT-FAI. My very first interview with these two comrades have shown me that they are on the "border-line" of Reformism. I had never met Oliver before, but I had met Federica in 1929. The change, since the Revolution swept her forward to the highest top-notch as leader, was only too apparent. I was strengthened in that impression every time I talked to her about the compromise she and others had made. It was too obvious to me that these comrades are working (sic) into the hands of the Soviet Government...I never saw a greater breach of faith with Anarchist principles than the joint "love-feast" of the CNT-FAI with the Russian satraps in Barcelona. It was a sight for the gods to see Garcia Oliver and the Russian Consul competing with each other in the glowing tribute to the Soviet government, or the eulogies that appeared daily in "Solidaridad Obrera"...I have not written about this to anyone, dear comrade, although I felt indignation and could have cried out my contempt of the so-called leaders of the CNT-FAI.

V.R.

FREEDOM PRESS CENTENARY VOLUMES

To mark the Centenary of 1986 of FREEDOM PRESS and of our journal *Freedom*, a special 88-page issue was published with the title: FREEDOM/ A HUNDRED YEARS/ October 1886 to October 1986.
as well as a series of volumes of selections from *Freedom* and the various journals published by FREEDOM PRESS. In some cases there will be supplements to the volumes. The present volume is a supplement to volume 2: *Spain 1936-39: Social Revolution and Counter-Revolution*

The other volumes in the series are:

Vol. 1 Selections from *Freedom* 1886 - 1936 (forthcoming)
Supplement: *Act For Yourselves!* by P. Kropotkin, 17 articles published 1886-1888 and now reprinted for the first time

Vol. 3 Selections from *War Commentary / Freedom* 1939-1950
Supplement: Neither East Nor West, articles by Marie Louise Berneri 1939-1947

Vol. 4 Selections from *Freedom* 1951 - 1964 (forthcoming)

Vol. 5 A Decade of Anarchy: Selections from the monthly journal *Anarchy* 1961-1970

Vol. 6 Selections from *Freedom* 1965-1986

This ambitious project has been made financially possible thanks to a substantial contribution to the Centenary issue of *Freedom* by FRIENDS OF FREEDOM PRESS LTD and by that long standing friend of FREEDOM PRESS, Hans Deichmann, for the volumes of Selections.

FREEDOM PRESS at present publish Freedom (fortnightly) and *The Raven* (quarterly) as well as some fifty anarchist titles. FREEDOM PRESS BOOKSHOP carries the most comprehensive stock of anarchist literature including titles from N. America. Please send for further particulars to:
FREEDOM PRESS
in Angel Alley
84b Whitechapel High Street
London E1 7QX

SPAIN 1936-39:
SOCIAL REVOLUTION
AND COUNTER REVOLUTION:
Selections from the anarchist fortnightly
Spain & the World

272 pages   0 900384 54 9   £5.00

*

LESSONS OF THE
SPANISH REVOLUTION
by
Vernon Richards

260 pages   0 900384 23 9   £4.00

FREEDOM PRESS in Angel Alley
84b Whitechapel High Street
London E1 7QX